MAKING IT
IN AMERICA

MAKING IT IN AMERICA

A 12-Point Plan for Growing Your

Business and Keeping Jobs at Home

JOHN BASSETT &
ELLIS HENICAN

CENTER
STREET®

NEW YORK   BOSTON   NASHVILLE

Center Street
Hachette Book Group
1290 Avenue of the Americas
New York, NY 10104
www.CenterStreet.com

Printed in the United States of America

RRD-C

First edition: May 2016

10 9 8 7 6 5 4 3 2 1

Book design by Timothy Shaner, NightandDayDesign.biz

Center Street is a division of Hachette Book Group, Inc.

The Center Street name and logo are trademarks of Hachette Book Group, Inc.

The Hachette Speakers Bureau provides a wide range of authors for speaking events. To find out more, go to www.HachetteSpeakersBureau.com or call (866) 376-6591.

The publisher is not responsible for websites (or their content) that are not owned by the publisher.

Library of Congress Control Number: 2016934146

ISBN: 978-1-4555-6355-5

To Pitty Pat

My bride of fifty-two wonderful years

Contents

Introduction

Stepping Up

I had never been inclined to turn away from struggle before. I wasn't about to turn away now.

Introduction

Stepping Up

I had never been inclined to turn away from struggle before. I wasn't about to turn away now.

I walked into the noisy finishing room at our sprawling factory in Galax, Virginia, and right away the conveyor belt stopped. Inside a furniture factory, silence is almost never a happy sound.

Uh-oh, I thought. *What's the problem here?*

All the workers were turning from their stations and were now walking toward me.

Was there a safety issue I hadn't heard about? Did somebody get hurt? Was there a problem with one of our machines? It had to be something fairly important. We'd worked hard to cut our downtime. In my long experience on factory floors, people don't usually *stop* working when the boss comes in.

Finishers do the messiest work in a furniture factory. The job requires speed, care, and genuine artistry. That conveyor runs fast, and if the stain is uneven or the lacquer's applied wrong, you've just spoiled the underlying craftsmanship. A sloppy finishing job is the first thing a dissatisfied customer will notice and complain about.

As the finishers crowded around me, I saw that no one was frowning. Nobody looked mad. Then a lady named Helen stepped up to speak for the group.

"John," she said, staring straight at me in her brown-stained coveralls. "We have something to tell you."

"Okay. What is it?"

"We see what you're going through," Helen said. "We see what you're trying to accomplish for us, and we want you to know one thing. You tell us what you need, and we're gonna do it for you. You tell us what you want, we'll get it done."

I heard her loud and clear. We were still struggling to save this factory and the seven hundred men and women it employed. Few people thought we'd be able to do it. We were the furniture industry's stubborn underdogs, hanging tough in southwest Virginia after most of our large competitors had shifted their production to new facilities overseas. Before Helen spoke, I'd been talking a good game but wasn't honestly sure we could achieve this long-shot American miracle. The moment she made that promise, I knew our competitors were the ones at a distinct disadvantage. We were absolutely going to survive.

I hugged the women, shook hands with the men, and said to them all, "Thank you. I know that. We can always count on each other."

After all we'd been through together—the reorganizations and the speed-ups, the sideways glances from the rest of the industry, the illegal dumping from low-wage foreign countries, all the new technology we'd implemented, the terrible sadness of watching neighboring factories close and good people get tossed from their jobs—I felt hugely grateful for the support I was getting from the floor. I knew Helen and the others weren't just blowing smoke or buttering me up. We were genuine partners here, the kinds of partners who were ready to take on the world together—and I meant that literally. I knew the employees had as much at stake as I did. Their whole futures were on the line.

"Okay," I said finally. "I have my first request."

"What is it?" they asked, as several of them stepped closer to hear.

"Get your butts back to work!" I said. "Let's get this line running! We gotta move some furniture!"

They laughed and clapped and quickly returned to the production line, moving freshly finished pieces of Vaughan-Bassett furniture out the factory door. As I headed to my desk upstairs to absorb what had just occurred, the workers were back at their stations and the finishing room was humming again.

DOING BUSINESS OUR WAY

My name is John D. Bassett III. Some call me JB3. I'm a third-generation Virginia furniture man. With my sons Doug and Wyatt, I run the largest wood bedroom furniture manufacturing plant in the United States. Which is kind of like running the busiest Chick-fil-A on Mars—there aren't too many others. But one, I keep discovering, can be a very powerful number. I've been described as driven, demanding, dedicated, profane, charming, iconoclastic, generous, and stubborn. Especially stubborn. Over the past three decades, our little company has been at the center of one of the epic battles of modern capitalism. We have weathered globalism, ever-changing technology, a crippling fiscal crisis, and profound industrial change. We stayed in America as virtually all our competitors rushed for the exits, shifting their production to high-volume factories in low-wage locations overseas. We were under enormous pressure to join the panicking stampede. But we refused to budge. We stuck with our people instead—their talent, their dedication, our history together, and the uncompromising quality of American workmanship. It's never been easy, but I am extremely glad we did.

It's the awesome power of one.

Our big bet on America has caused quite a stir in our industry and beyond. Some people are still shaking their heads at us. They can't imagine why we didn't just roll with the tide. But to many, our company has come to symbolize the strong fighting spirit that still burns inside the American worker, despite all the forces busily trying to snuff that spirit out. People say we're a much-needed antidote to all the defeatist talk they keep hearing. The way I see it, we are living, breathing proof that dedicated management and loyal employees, working together as a team in this great country of ours, can hold their own against anyone anywhere and achieve just about anything!

That's the story of our company, our furniture, and our dreams. Born in America. Made in America. Stayed in America. I don't think we should ever have to leave.

If I sound patriotic, it's because I am. America has been hugely generous to me and my family. American workers and American consumers made "Bassett" one of the most famous names in furniture and turned many of my relatives into multimillionaires. I wasn't about to walk away from that legacy and that long-standing debt. Growing up in the time and place that I did, I was taught values that have always stuck with me: The worth of a dollar. The joy of quality workmanship. The need to look out for those less fortunate. The importance of treating people fairly and decently. Those lessons were reinforced by my experience in the United States Army serving on the German border. The call of duty and honor. The need to apply myself. The fact that America is still worth defending. The knowledge that our freedoms and beliefs stand for something special all around the world. I had never been inclined to turn away from struggle before, and I wasn't about to turn away now.

How we are pulling this off—finding the right strategy, getting the best out of our employees, building a product that people find desirable—is an important story and an inspiring one. It features some wonderful characters and some unexpected twists. It couldn't be more timely than it is right now, as America is readjusting to an increasingly dicey international terrain and a rapidly changing world economy.

To get to where we are, we had to ignore the constant prodding of respected experts. We stood up to sweeping business trends no one thought we had a chance against. We beat a fresh path through a thicket of obstacles and obfuscation while others gave up.

The results have been immensely gratifying. We rescued an American factory. We saved an American town. We preserved hundreds of jobs in a proud American community—jobs people really depended on. We doubled down on America just as others were boarding Air China flights to Beijing. We kept building well-crafted American furniture at a time when fewer and fewer people even tried.

We had something all the top experts and their holy spreadsheets could never quantify. We had people on our side. Decent, hardworking, dedicated people who simply refused to fail. The most underused asset in America today is not technology. It's not political power. It's not the Internet. It's people working together as a team. We've all got to learn to energize our people and get the most from everyone.

With the right kind of leadership, one company really can change the world.

THE RIGHT STRATEGY FOR CHALLENGING TIMES

In her bestselling book, *Factory Man,* author Beth Macy told the story of the rise and near-collapse of American furniture manufacturing and the bold path followed by our feisty firm. (She did call me an "asshole"—twice on the first page of chapter 1! I've chosen to overlook that because, on the very same page, she also described me as a "larger-than-life rule breaker who for more than a decade has stood almost single-handed against the outflow of furniture from America." I guess that's what writers call "a balanced portrayal.")

Making It in America is the story of *how* we managed to accomplish all this—in all its step-by-step, practical detail. In the pages that follow, I will reveal exactly what it took. Relying on my decades of business experience, I will take you inside our private thinking and our fresh leadership approach. I will describe the heartfelt values and modern business tactics that helped us surprise everyone. Most important of all, I will explain how you can apply our people-first leadership to any competitive challenge you might confront. For the first time ever, I will lay out my Ten-Point Plan for Growing Your Business and Keeping Jobs at Home. These are principles that have guided us from beginning to end. I don't know where we'd be without them, and I'm certain you'll find them valuable, whatever business you are in. They are battle-tested and clearly understandable. They are flexible, scalable, and ready to go. They are effective whether you're managing a smoothie stand in a strip mall or a far-flung conglomerate.

1. The power of a winning attitude
2. The importance of treating people like something more than numbers
3. Transparent leadership
4. Facing the tough decisions
5. The willingness to change (again and again and again)
6. The refusal to panic
7. Communication, teamwork, and why they fuel each other

8. The need to keep investing in the future
9. Making the best of the worst situations
10. The huge impact of buying American

If you can get your head around these concepts and follow the steps I describe, they will change your business life forever, as they have fundamentally changed mine. It's not just Vaughan-Bassett. It's not just the furniture industry. It's any business, anywhere. We're making it in America, *and so can you*!

If taken to heart, our approach will save jobs, lift profits, enrich communities, boost the economy, and expand opportunities for everyone—from the shop floor to the tech lab to the office cubicle to the service center to the executive suite. If we can do it in our company, you can do it in yours. Whatever challenges your business is facing, whatever resources you have at your command, you just need the right people and the right approach with them. If we can all just pull together, there is no limit to what we can achieve.

LET THE JOURNEY BEGIN

I am often inspired by the wise voices of history. I spend a lot of time listening to them.

As I was starting on this journey, some special words were planted firmly in my head, focusing me, energizing me, and reminding me of how much I owed the country I loved.

They were the words of a young president, delivered January 20, 1961, a frigid Friday in Washington, D.C., as I was away in the U.S. Army. John F. Kennedy had just taken the oath of office on the steps of the U.S. Capitol and was addressing the American people for the first time as their president. Everywhere you looked, the world was facing danger at least as severe as today's. The rush of the arms race. The height of the Cold War. An increasingly bellicose Soviet Union. People had much to feel anxious about. Whatever the new president said that day, it had to be strong.

His message arrived on tall shoulders. Kennedy's speechwriter, Ted Sorensen, had been studying President Abraham Lincoln's Gettysburg Address and the oratory of other presidents at especially perilous times. Since election night, the president-elect had been consulting with some of the smartest people he knew, including former presidential candidate Adlai Stevenson II and Harvard economist John Kenneth Galbraith. But historians say his real inspiration came decades earlier during the future president's prep school days at the Choate School in Wallingford, Connecticut, where the importance of giving, not just taking, was the credo of longtime headmaster Seymour St. John.

The speech that day was one of the shortest inaugural addresses ever delivered by a U.S. president, thirteen minutes and thirty seconds from the first word to the last, not counting the long ovation at the end. But the president's remarks quickly took their place among the greatest orations of American history. It was Kennedy's belief that America could no longer rely solely on its military might to keep the world safe and prosperous. A strong military was vital, he believed. But America also had to lead with diplomacy and help lift other nations in need. Sometimes, he was convinced, it was crucial to do right for the sake of the common good.

"In the long history of the world," he said that day, "only a few generations have been granted the role of defending freedom in its hour of maximum danger." Notice the optimistic spin? These aren't burdens. These are opportunities. We have been "granted" this special role. Kennedy's goal, as mine would later be, was to motivate Americans, not to frighten them.

"And so, my fellow Americans," the young president finally declared, "ask not what your country can do for you. Ask what you can do for your country."

I was moved by those words the first time I heard them while serving in the army in Germany. They have stayed with me ever since. But what do they mean exactly? What is it we owe this country of ours? Our freedom isn't free, of course, and America isn't America without the support and commitment of its citizens. We can't just take from our country. We also have to give.

This land we live in is the greatest democracy ever and the most admired country on earth. What are our responsibilities in return? Frankly, on most days we aren't asked to do much. Pay our taxes, follow the law, and not much else. We enjoy an extraordinary level of freedom. We live fairly comfortable lives. We have to work for a living, and many people do feel pressed financially—given the cost of living today and the lifestyles we seek to maintain. But we have a history of long prosperity, the benefits of amazing technology, and the pleasures of nearly endless diversions and entertainment. We have no military draft anymore. In our country, people are not forced to serve if they don't care to. When I grew up, my three brothers-in-law and I all went into the military. One went to the U.S. Naval Academy at Annapolis. The other three of us went to civilian colleges, but we all started our adulthoods in uniform. Some American families still have that connection to the military, but the vast majority do not.

As a business leader, it seems to me we have to do something more than reduce labor costs, avoid taxes, produce as cheaply as possible, and maximize our margins regardless of the human cost. What kind of legacy is that? Running lean and earning profits are certainly important business aims, but they aren't the only goals great leaders have. We must owe something more to the country that has been so generous to us. As President Kennedy reminded us more than half a century ago, we also have to give. We have to produce valuable products. We have to create decent jobs. We have to support the communities we live and work in. We have to boost the nation's economy, lift the tide for everyone, and willingly pay our fair share. You don't hear so much about that anymore from today's bottom-line consultants and business school experts. But those are the values that made America a great place to live and gave us the strongest economy the world has ever seen.

Somehow or another, those of us in business have to protect and nourish this national miracle of ours—and still make profits as we do.

When I'm gone, I want to be known as someone who cared about his people. I want everyone, not just those at the top, to do well. I want to leave the nation I love with stronger communities, better jobs, greater companies, a keener work ethic, and more security than when I arrived. The only way that will happen is if we focus more on each other's needs and achievements. That's where my principles really kick in.

It's never easy, but that is what this journey of ours is all about. Each of us has the power to make this happen. Stick with me here. The rewards can be extraordinary.

Chapter 1

Learning to Lead

I absorbed the most important thing the army had to offer a young officer like me: a chance to lead. The officer I admired most was my captain, Ray Teel. "Learn the principles of leadership," he told me. "Learn discipline. Learn that once an order is given, it's time to execute. Don't just sit around. Get it done!" He was a real mentor to me. A couple of things quickly became clear. Don't ask someone to do something you aren't willing to do yourself. If you want a young soldier to get up out of a foxhole and charge into battle knowing he can get his butt killed, you'd better be there beside him.

I wasn't a born leader. No one is. I squeezed the lessons of leadership out of life's experiences one by one across the decades. I've been learning to lead since I was a child. My family gets credit for some of it. The U.S. Army gets credit for more. And the wrenching struggles of a great American industry taught me some dangerous pitfalls to avoid. I'm not always the quickest learner, but I learn.

Growing up as John D. Bassett III in Bassett, Virginia, I could never just blend in. Not when the Bassett family was so deeply rooted in the hills of southwest Virginia. Not when the Bassett Furniture Industries was the lifeblood of the local economy, not to mention a major American manufacturing concern. My grandfather, the original John D. Bassett, ran the company. Then my uncle Bill took over, and my father after that. I was surrounded by Bassetts everywhere. Anything I did, from the day I climbed out of the playpen and toddled across the room, was immediately known by everyone.

We were a good Baptist family and attended the Pocahontas Bassett Baptist Church, named after my grandmother, Pocahontas Bassett. In the Baptist church where I grew up, we didn't even have wine for communion—it was grape juice. The local Baptists had a rigid sense of right and wrong, and no one ever seemed confused about the difference. While I have since become an Episcopalian (they have more fun!), I still have my mother's voice bouncing in my head: "To whom much is given, much is expected in return. You have an obligation to this community."

I didn't quite know quite what she was driving at then, but I could tell she was talking about me.

They had a similar attitude at Riverside Military Academy in Gainesville, Georgia, where I was sent for three years of prep school, skipping John D. Bassett High. Situated on beautiful Lake Lanier in the foothills of the Blue Ridge Mountains, military school was supposed to instill some discipline in me. My parents thought I was on the road to delinquency. How delinquent could I have been? I lived in a town where everyone knew me. I worked every summer in the family business, up at 5:15 a.m. and straight to the factory floor. I wasn't into drugs or alcohol or any of that stuff. I recognized where the line was, and I never got caught on the wrong side of it. But my parents had their concerns, so there I was, 350 miles from home, in a neatly pressed uniform, marching with a rifle in the blazing Georgia sun. We were expected to make our beds and put our rooms in proper order. Everything else just flowed from there. We had to file our rifles. We had close-order drill. We were required to show up on time. We learned to follow orders and live to a certain standard because that standard was right. The school was all about order and discipline. Some of the instructors there made the hometown Baptists look like liberal-minded Unitarians.

Not surprisingly, that kind of upbringing had a real effect on me. It gave me a sense of belonging. It made me accustomed to getting along in a tightly controlled environment. It also taught me that wherever we come from, we are all judged by what we do. After Riverside I went off to college at Washington and Lee University. W&L is a wonderful institution of higher learning. Nestled in Lexington, Virginia, there is glorious history everywhere you look. Founded in 1796 and endowed in part by George Washington, the school was renamed for the first American president and General Robert E. Lee, who served as the college president until his death in 1870. I wish I could have a do-over. I didn't pay much attention the first time around. College was where I discovered alcohol and girls and the many ways a young man can have fun. I did join the ROTC. After military school, I knew I could handle that. I spent the summer after my junior year at Fort Knox, Kentucky, returning to campus in time for my senior year. Immediately upon graduation, I was commissioned as a second lieutenant in the United States Army.

It was 1959. The Cold War was going full blast, and I was sent to Germany with the Fourteenth Armored Cavalry Regiment—that means tanks. At twenty-two years old I began commanding a reconnaissance platoon. Decades later, the whole free world would celebrate when the Berlin Wall came down. I was there in 1961 when the Berlin Wall went up, a physical barrier dividing the communist east from the democratic west.

JOHN WHO?

I loved being away. While in the army, I was out of Bassett, Virginia, in a place where the name John Bassett didn't mean anything to anybody. No one in Germany knew who the hell I was. The German girls found me charming, and I had friends from everywhere. What wasn't to like?

My father promised if I quit smoking for a year, he would give me two thousand dollars. The year was up, I was still in Germany, and he wanted to put the money in the bank.

"No, no, no," I said. "Send me the two thousand dollars."

I took the money, added some of my own, and bought a white

Porsche with a red leather interior. In the summertime, the hardtop came off and was replaced with a black canvas cover. That automobile was almost an unfair advantage with the German girls!

Just fifteen years earlier, the German government had been our sworn enemy. Now many of its citizens seemed to cherish us as their liberators, grateful for how we'd helped defeat the Nazis and set the German people free. They also appreciated that we stood between them and the Russians.

Returning from maneuvers late one winter afternoon, one of our tanks broke down. We pulled up to a guesthouse, our full thirty-man platoon. A heavyset grandmotherly woman said we could leave our vehicles in the parking lot. She got on the telephone, and suddenly half a dozen other older German ladies arrived. They locked the gates of the guesthouse and began to cook. We had a huge meal of pork schnitzel, spaetzle, and applesauce before we all went off to bed.

After an eggs-and-sausage breakfast, I tried to pay for the fine German hospitality. She wouldn't accept anything. Her son had been in the German army, she said, and was captured by the Americans and held as a prisoner of war. After VE Day, he came back home, healthy and happy that the war was over. "He was wearing better clothes than when he left me," his mother said. "This is for taking care of my son."

My time in Germany wasn't all schnitzel and sports cars. The East German army, backed by the Soviet Union, had watchtowers on their side of the border and a ten-meter strip of land that was seeded with mines. Stationed twenty miles away, my squadron patrolled ninety miles of the hardened border with a forward observation post. We were required to have one officer there at all times.

Since I was a bachelor, I ended up with a lot of that sentry duty, staring into the abyss of communism.

There was a constant flow of East German citizens willing to risk their lives to escape to freedom. Watching them try was a life-changing experience. I saw a father and young son manage to get across on a motorcycle. I helped a fleeing family get to the West German authorities and begin a new life. Another time, I was at my border post on a bright, crisp morning, when a teenage girl, fourteen or fifteen years old, came running toward the line. I could clearly see her coming, her eyes focused straight ahead. If that young girl had made it across the border, we could have protected her. But we weren't allowed to cross the line into East Germany, and she was stopped just a few yards shy of the border. The East German soldiers opened fire, and that girl collapsed in a bloody puddle on the ground.

I was never the same after watching that happen. "The only reason you are here is because you were born in America," I said to myself. "You are damn lucky." That's the moment I understood the army could provide me with opportunities to do more than flirt with blond girls.

LESSONS LEARNED IN UNIFORM

I absorbed the most important thing the army had to offer a young officer like me: a chance to lead. The officer I admired most was my captain, Ray Teel. "Learn the principles of leadership," he told me. "Learn discipline. Learn that once an order is given, it's time to execute. Don't just sit around. Get it done!" He was a real mentor to me.

A couple of things quickly became clear. Don't ask someone to do something you aren't willing to do yourself. If you want a young soldier to get up out of a foxhole and charge into battle knowing he can get his butt killed, you'd better be there beside him.

Perhaps the most valuable lesson I learned was how vital it is to inspire respect in those you lead. It's nice if the people you lead like you or want to be your friends, but that's not what matters in the end. People want leaders they respect, whose commitment and competence they believe in.

General Dwight Eisenhower was a brilliant leader, and people greatly admired him. General George Patton was a brilliant leader, and I think it's fair to say he wasn't always so well liked. But he was certainly respected. People respected the devil out of him. They knew Patton was totally committed to victory, and the man unquestionably knew how to fight a war.

When everything is running smoothly, when everyone feels well cared for and the organization is meeting all its goals, any dumb-ass can be an effective leader. Good leaders prove themselves when times are bad. We have a huge admiration for presidents who lead us through difficult situations—Washington, Lincoln, Franklin Roosevelt, and other true greats. We should also be grateful to the ones who kept us out of trouble. Thank you, President Eisenhower! From 1952 to 1960, the tensest part of the Cold War, America was not involved in another major conflict. Eisenhower must have been doing something right. As a general, he'd already demonstrated the ability to run a massive military campaign. As president, he proved he could avoid being entangled in one. That's worth admiring.

After the Russians built the Berlin Wall, President Kennedy extended all U.S. service members' duty for another year. A lot of my buddies were upset about that—they couldn't wait to return home. As for me, I wasn't ready to leave. The extension felt like a gift to me. I was promoted to first lieutenant and wasn't rushing to go anywhere. I happily stayed in Germany a full three years.

BACK HOME, A NEW MAN

When I returned to Bassett, Virginia, in 1962, I went to work full-time in the family business a far more focused young man. It's amazing what a few years away can do. Even though my grandfather started the company, I didn't automatically inherit a fancy title right off the bat. I was in a roll-up-my-sleeves frame of mind. I started as a utility troubleshooter. I wasn't sent to the plants that were doing well and making profits. I was the turnaround guy. I went to the factories that were having problems, like the J.D. plant in Bassett and later the National/Mt. Airy plant in Andy Griffith's North Carolina hometown, Mount Airy. I liked the variety and enjoyed the leadership challenge. I liked showing up with my legal pad and figuring out what was wrong. Sometimes, I'd make a list of three hundred issues, then I'd pick out six or eight that needed immediate attention and add another three or four crises every day. There was always something to improve.

Because of my army training, I knew what to do. Many managers spend too much time working to contain problems instead of solving them. That's wrong. Find the pattern that's causing the problem and do what it takes to fix it. Most issues, I've discovered, can be traced to poorly performing personnel. Even if there's an equipment problem or a facilities problem, it can usually be attributed to someone. So replace the cabinet room foreman if that's what it takes. By moving him, forty other problems might also disappear, and he may very well perform better elsewhere.

The September I returned to the States, I met a popular sophomore at Hollins College in Roanoke. Patricia Exum came from a furniture family, too. Her grandfather, Bunyan Vaughan, had worked for my grandfather. In 1919, with my grandfather's seed money, her grandfather opened his own company, Vaughan-Bassett Furniture. It was a rapid success.

Pat was a busy girl. When I met her, she had plans for the next three Friday and Saturday nights. So we went out on Sunday and again on Tuesday evening. We got secretly engaged just before Christmas over juicy rib-eye steaks at the Shenandoah Club. We told no one until Pat came for a visit with my family after the holidays.

During that visit, my mother brought out a stack of bills I'd run up on my parents' account at the Shenandoah Club. To deflect her complaints about my spending, I said, "I have something to tell you."

"What is it?"

"I'm not gonna get hooked up with any of those German girls," I said. "Pat and I are engaged." The Shenandoah Club bills never came up again.

Pat and I were married the next August. Doug was the firstborn. Then along came Wyatt and then Fran, and I was finally feeling like a grown-up. I had a remarkable wife, three lovely children, and an interesting career in an ever-changing industry that could trace its roots back a couple of hundred years.

A FAMILY BUSINESS, A ROARING INDUSTRY

American furniture making began just about the time America did, with a scattering of self-taught craftsmen working alone or in tiny shops, building beds, chests, and tables for a young, pioneer nation that needed somewhere to sleep more comfortable than a bedroll and somewhere to sit less backbreaking than a circle of stones around a fire.

As the industrial revolution took hold, hundreds of furniture factories sprang up in America. In the 1800s they were mostly up north in places like Michigan and upstate New York. In the early 1900s, furniture manufacturing migrated south, especially to North Carolina, Virginia, and Tennessee, where the timber was plentiful and the hardscrabble mountain people had talent with their hands.

My relatives were part of that glorious wave. In 1902, my father's father, John D. Bassett Sr., with his brother and brother-in-law, turned a local sawmill into the most successful furniture maker on earth, The Bassett Furniture Industries of Bassett, Virginia, and spawned numerous other companies and business enterprises. They and their competitors shipped boxcars of furniture across the continent. Those businesses kept dozens of southern towns prosperous and generations of local people gainfully employed, often from the time they left school until they grew too old to walk to work.

At its peak, from the years just after World War II into the 1960s and 1970s, the furniture industry employed more than a hundred thousand men and women who produced millions of pieces of furniture a year. Conditions were almost ideal for such an industry.

The U.S. population was soaring. The economy was booming through those postwar decades. People were moving from small rental apartments into larger, single-family homes. The American suburbs were developing and spreading farther and farther out from the nation's downtowns. If the American Dream included owning a nice home for the family, that home had to be filled with decent furniture, ideally bearing the Bassett name. You couldn't invite the neighbors over and expect them to sit cross-legged on the floor!

As the demand increased, the southern furniture makers kept getting better at what they did. The factories were becoming more mechanized. The production lines were speeding up. All the big companies, ours included, were producing multiple product lines, something for every conceivable taste—from traditional to transitional to modern to avant-garde—and something at every imaginable price point. By 1970, more than one-quarter of U.S. employees worked in manufacturing jobs. Furniture, in those years, was a great business to be part of.

I learned my profession from all the companies I worked with and a lot of generous furniture people I met along the way. But those early years at The Bassett Furniture Industries were the ones that taught me the most. That company didn't only teach me. It paid for my mistakes when I was learning my moves and building up my confidence. Everyone needs an early employer like that. I will always owe the people there a great deal of appreciation. They really did prepare me for the rest of my professional life.

The Smith River runs through Bassett, Virginia. I like to say I got my real education on the banks of the Smith River. But by late 1982, it was becoming obvious that I wasn't going to realize my dream of running The Bassett Furniture Industries. My sister's husband, Bob Spilman, was in charge at that point, and he showed no sign of expanding my role. If I were going to grade myself a success, I concluded, I would have to do something different.

So I resigned.

I told my brother-in-law, "I don't want to die as JDB Senior's grandson, as Doug Bassett's son, or Bob Spilman's brother-in-law. I might die a failure, but I will die my own failure. And I have decided I'm willing to take that risk."

The timing seemed right. Our older son, Doug, was going off to college. Wyatt was a junior in high school, and Fran was just leaving for boarding school. What would I do next?

Twice before, Pat's uncle Buck Higgins had asked me to run Vaughan-Bassett. Twice I had told him no. Now my wife was encouraging me to reopen that possibility. "They keep offering you this job," she said. "It's a family company. Why don't you think about taking it?" She had a point.

GETTING TO WORK

When I got to Vaughan-Bassett, my title was VP/Plant Manager. I looked closely at the operations and realized this was another troubleshooting assignment for me. From inside, things were much worse than they looked from the outside. The company was losing money. Business was painfully slow. The factory was operating one week on and one week off. Invoices were not being paid on time. I knew I could figure out what was needed. We needed the right people, and I needed to get to work. This was a military operation as much as anything I had faced in Germany.

During the first year or so, we replaced factory management. We bought some new machines. We hired Duke Taylor from National/Mt. Airy, a brilliant, hands-on plant operator I'd gotten to know when I ran that factory. Duke had high standards. He was difficult to please, but he made it his relentless mission to improve the quality of our factory output.

"We have the worst quality engineering I have ever seen," Duke complained in a moment of high frustration in the summer of 1983. We'd been jobbing out our engineering work, and Duke didn't like it one bit.

"We've gotta have Linda," he said.

Linda McMillan was the engineer at National/Mt. Airy. She was headstrong and quirky but remarkably talented. She was at least as headstrong as Duke. She had no formal training, entirely self-taught. She was the best our industry had. She was also one of the few women in the engineering side of the furniture business.

I knew she'd be expensive, but Duke had already thought of that. "You and I are gonna pay her out of our pockets," he said matter-of-factly—"until the company can afford her."

We still had to convince Linda. "You'll have all the freedom you need," I assured her when Duke brought her by to talk with me. "We'll tell you what we're looking for. You'll draw it. We'll build it like you say. If you come over here, you can do it your way."

That's what she wanted to hear. "I have faith," she said, "and you have the team."

There was some initial resistance in the machine room. I wasn't sure how much of the issue was because Linda was a woman or how much was the quiet resolve she exuded. On occasion if something was cut wrong, I would hear some grumbling in the machine room. "Linda didn't draw it right," someone might say.

"That's unlikely" was my stock answer. "Go cut it again." Somehow the issue disappeared.

With Duke and Linda working together, we had a pair of geniuses on the floor. She could engineer it, and he could execute it. There was nothing those two couldn't achieve. Even our crises were opportunities for them. Our much-anticipated Elvis Presley Collection (the "Love Me Tender" bed, the "Burning Love" mirror, the "Graceland" armoire with optional frosted-glass door edged with etched musical notes and Elvis's signature) fell flat at the worst possible moment. Go figure! I went to Duke and Linda and said to them: "If we're gonna keep this factory open, you have two weeks to come up with something new." Instead of saying, "No, we can't do it," they said, "Yes, we can." They pulled it off just in time. With her drawing it up and Duke getting it out, they saved our year. We were off and running again.

THE LEADER'S ACTION PLAN: CHAPTER 1

WHAT LEADERS LEARN

APPRECIATE WHAT YOU'VE BEEN BLESSED WITH, THEN BUILD ON IT. Everyone gets something. I got love, security, education, and an inside ticket to a fascinating American industry. That left me poised to succeed. Over time, I came to see that I had to prove what *I* was capable of. No one could do that for me. Everyone in business—and in life—follows some similar path. What you are given is only a start.

LOOK AT EVERY EXPERIENCE AS A LEARNING OPPORTUNITY. You'll be glad you did. Your family, your education, your early career, your colleagues, and your competitors—they all teach something you need to learn. In my younger days, I learned the importance of treating people decently and doing things right. You'll learn your own lessons if you pay attention. I don't know where I'd be without mine.

IDENTIFY PEOPLE YOU ADMIRE, AND COPY WHAT YOU LIKE. From leaders like army captain Ray Teel I learned the lessons of leadership. The men didn't have to love you. They didn't even have to like you. It was all about respect, those you led believing you were in there with them and always had their backs. Achieve that, and you can lead anyone. Find role models you admire, and take their talents to heart.

SEEK TALENT EVERYWHERE. A lot of people would not have put a self-taught, headstrong woman in charge of engineering at a major furniture company. That was one of the smarter decisions I ever made. Always try to judge people on what they are capable of, not what you've heard others say. You miss a lot of great talent making the conventional choices every time.

Chapter 2

Killer
Competition

Was the competition really that ruthless? Were American factory owners really as greedy as my Chinese dinner companion claimed? I hated to admit it. But many of them never even paused to consider, "Isn't there some way we can compete here in America? Don't we have some advantages the foreigners don't? Do we really want to walk away from so much knowledge and experience?" Scared they'd be trampled in the rush to the bottom, many of these American companies never even put up a fight. "What choice do we have?" many of my old friends and competitors said.

Have you ever had someone tell you something you didn't want to hear—but the second you heard it, you knew it was the honest-to-God truth? That's what happened to me one boozy night in Hong Kong more than three decades ago. Never before had a competitor revealed himself so openly. Never since have I had any doubt about what American business is up against.

Everyone knew everyone in the U.S. furniture industry. We'd always maintained friendly relations with our various competitors. Most of us lived in North Carolina or Virginia. We'd run into each other in local restaurants, on the golf course, or at church. Our kids and grandkids went to school together and played on the same Little League teams. The whole industry got together at the High Point Market trade show for a week every fall and spring, meeting buyers, trading gossip, and showing our new lines. There were unspoken rules of engagement, as there are in many industries, and hardly anyone violated them. We competed energetically. We tried to sell more furniture than the other guys. We pushed our products, launched new promotions, and did what we could to expand our own slices of the marketplace. We even teamed up from time to time to combat common threats like rising showroom rents or the latest environmental regulation coming down from Washington.

So there I was, on a fact-finding tour of Asian manufacturing plants, learning what they might be capable of and how their costs compared to ours. Vaughan-Bassett, like many other American furniture makers in the mid-1980s, was trying to figure how globalization would fit into our business models. We were looking to see if Asia was going to be the next big thing—and, if so, how our companies might be affected.

I had finished a long day of meetings in Taiwan. A plant manager had given me an extensive factory tour with a pretty young translator tagging along. He showed off his gleaming new equipment and his rows of neatly attired employees, who never seemed to look up from their work. He told me how much more efficient they were than Americans. Later that night, the owner and I sat down for dinner at Hong Kong's lavish Peninsula hotel. Actually, it was more like a feast. The food was spectacular: six full courses—vegetable spring rolls, oyster pancakes, minced pork rice, a whole cuttlefish, a spicy hot pot, and moon cakes with red bean paste for dessert— all washed down with bottles of very nice French wine and shot glasses of a clear, sticky after-dinner liqueur that I believe was made from sorghum. I'm not saying the man was drunk, but the wine and liqueur definitely seemed to have loosened him up a little. Something did. In the afterglow of all that consumption, he leaned back on a chaise, casually puffed on a cigar, and began to speak. He said something that our translator did not repeat.

He said it again, more emphatically the second time. Still, not a word in English.

"He wants to tell me something," I prompted the translator. Only then did she repeat the factory owner's words.

"We have done business with people from every part of the world," the man said. "But we have never met anyone as greedy as the Americans—or as naïve."

Really? Greedy *and* naïve? That didn't sound like most of the Americans I knew, the ones I'd attended school with, gone to church with, served in the army with, played golf with, and was acquainted with in a hundred different ways. They were almost uniformly good and decent human beings who cared about their country and their communities and their families. They strived to do good work. But clearly, that wasn't this man's impression.

"If the price is right," he continued, "you will do *anything,* even give up your businesses. Only the Americans will do that."

Then he made a prediction to me—or was it a promise? It definitely sounded ominous. "When we get on top," he said, "don't expect us to be dumb enough to do for you what you have been dumb enough to do for us."

As I sat at that dinner table seven thousand miles from home, I remembered an old Latin expression: *In vino, veritas*—in wine, there is truth. Thank God for that. If this was going to be the next big thing in our industry—proud American companies having their furniture built overseas—we were better off knowing the kind of competition we were about to face, even if we didn't like the sound of it. I vowed then and there that I would never forget what I heard that night in Hong Kong, and I can promise you I've not.

TOUGHER THAN IT'S EVER BEEN

Competition. More competition. Tougher competition than ever before. That's the story of the business world over the past three decades as technology raced ahead and globalism gained an increasingly powerful grip. It's true regardless of what industry you are advancing, whatever profession you have chosen to pursue. The challenges are tougher. The competitors are more ruthless. The victories are harder fought. It isn't enough today to run a good company or build a strong product or have loyal customers or dream up a world-changing idea. It's not enough to provide a vital service or a popular product better than anyone else has been able to. Those are just the basic costs of entry. There's so much more to juggle now. The marketplace is constantly shifting. Costs keep rising. Tastes keep changing. The technology that saves us this morning can make us obsolete tomorrow afternoon. Marketing. Branding. Advertising. PR. Benefit packages and training regiments. Accounting procedures, tax strategies, and sales software. And don't forget the constant human resource issues. The questions go on and on. How are you keeping the vendors happy? How tight is your distribution chain? What's your digital strategy or your mobile platform? It's enough to make anyone's head spin. No wonder people in business feel stressed!

It isn't just the intensity of the competition that's been rising. So has the diversity and sheer number of competitors. There's a nearly infinite number of people just waiting to move in and pounce. If you're in retail, it used to be you had to worry about the store around the corner and maybe the one across town. Now, thanks to Amazon and FedEx and all their busy cousins, local brick-and-mortar outlets are only a slice of the landscape. In this age of universal e-tailing and easy mouse clicks, your direct, sale-by-sale competitors include anyone anywhere whose brand name pops up in a Google search. When these competitors look at you, all they see are customers ripe for poaching. And retailers aren't the only ones getting squeezed. Something similar is happening in every field. If you provide a service or build a product or advise someone else, you constantly have to wonder: Could my customers be lured away by a brash new player in the local market or a lower-cost competitor in Botswana, Bosnia, or Bangalore?

Often, the greatest threats seem to come out of nowhere. Someone has a new product line you didn't think of. Someone has a vendor relationship that gives a special edge. Someone has a marketing plan that is suddenly striking a chord. Someone has a way to save money on manufacturing costs that could actually be the death of us all.

Don't ever say it doesn't matter who wins and who loses in today's competitive environment. So much today hangs on our ability to compete. Our companies. Our careers. Our employees. The families who depend on us. The communities we live and work in. Companies that don't survive don't send anyone's kids to college. They don't provide a single employee with somewhere to go in the morning or fill the empty storefronts on a single Main Street. Even our nation's position in the world depends in large measure on how we—and millions of others like us—are able to compete.

FACTORY ASIA

I've been especially focused on the threat of Factory Asia, the name that's been given to the region's complex of low-wage factories, easily corrupted governments, and cross-border supply chains. Asia first emerged as a manufacturing power in the 1960s when Japan began exporting electronics and consumer goods. Soon enough, Taiwan and South Korea followed Japan's lead, quickly scooping up a share of the low-end U.S. market.

American businesspeople often sneered at the Asian producers, convinced their products were of questionable quality. "Made in Japan" was somewhere between an insult and a punch line. But the Asian producers were just learning to compete effectively, and few

American businesspeople had any idea how tenacious these new competitors could be. By the 1980s Japanese firms were building plants across Southeast Asia, and China was beginning to open up.

That change happened gradually, in fits and starts. President Richard Nixon made his historic journey to China in 1972, preaching the values of free markets, international engagement, and modern capitalism. Communist Party chairman Mao Zedong, who'd held an iron grip on China since 1945, finally died in 1976. His successors were far more interested in competing with the West than in maintaining Mao-style isolation and ideological purity. And the world's most populous nation began to create its own, unique version of cowboy capitalism. That was the real Factory Asia game-changer.

In 1990, the region accounted for 26.5 percent of global manufacturing output. By 2013 that share had reached 46.5 percent. Today China accounts for half of Asia's output. The region's share of global trade in intermediate inputs—the goods that are eventually pieced together into final products—rose from 14 percent in 2000 to 50 percent in 2012, and it is rising still. All this brought fresh competitive pressure to American firms.

Low-cost Chinese importer or high-tech Silicon Valley start-up, the tougher our competition gets, the better we have to be. No matter who we're competing against—other companies, other leaders, even our own past achievements—we can't take anything for granted. The stakes are too high. The issues are too large and too personal.

It's no time for business leaders to panic or freeze or feel confused. This is a time for boldness, creativity, and constant teamwork. You can sit back and wait for the tide to wash over you. Or you can act.

JUST CRUISING ALONG AND . . .

A s the years rolled on, Vaughan-Bassett stayed busy building our future and looking for opportunities to expand. In 1986 we put a partnership together to buy the bankrupt Williams furniture plant in Sumter, South Carolina—one-third for Vaughan-Bassett, one-third for a local Sumter investor group, one-third for me. We renamed the operation V-B/Williams. Pat's uncle was still the CEO of Vaughan-Bassett. The factory in Galax was securely in Duke and Linda's hands. This factory in Sumter gave me a chance to run something on my own.

When I showed up there, the entire staff was three security guards and a woman in personnel. I was determined to make something of this place, and I'd had enough experience working in family-run businesses to know what to do. We started hiring, and in early 1987 our first pieces of furniture came down the line and into a box. The company was profitable in sixty days. We replaced a lot of equipment, improved the facilities, and gradually got employment up to 350. It was a wonderful experience and a real confidence booster.

Now, *that's* building a business!

Never get too comfortable, right? Two years later, Hurricane Hugo blew the whole place to smithereens. What did we do? We didn't walk away. Within forty-eight hours, we had people sleeping in trailers and planning our return. In seventy-two hours, we were building the plant back and replacing a roof. We were back in production ten days after the storm.

By the early 1990s, I was Vaughan-Bassett's CEO, and we kept seeking new opportunities, building our furniture, serving our customers, looking after our employees, and competing with the same family-owned companies we always had. Globalization was beginning to have some effect, but nothing we couldn't stand up against when—*wham*! The spattering of imported product we'd been seeing in the market turned into an industry-changing avalanche. It wasn't just a factory here or there. It was furniture plants all across Asia, contracting with American companies to shift their production overseas, cutting American workers entirely out of the equation, and pulverizing another chunk of the American economy.

Were American factory owners really as greedy as my dinner companion in Hong Kong had claimed? Would they really sell out their own employees and their own businesses in search of the next low-cost manufacturing opportunity in some distant corner of the world? Actually, it was even worse than that.

It was on another trip to Asia, this one in 2002, that I finally came to see the full dimensions of the threat racing toward us. I was visiting China's industrial northeast, outside the gritty factory city of Dalian, not far from North Korea. Though it was only late November, a stiff breeze was already whipping off the Yellow Sea. But that wasn't what stung the most. It was the words of the politically connected factory owner I was meeting with.

"Mr. Bassett," he said to me, as soon as I sat in a chair in front of his desk. "We would like to make all your furniture for you."

There was no lavish dinner this time, no sweet after-dinner drinks, no Peninsula hotel. Just a few of us in a spare office, listening as he boldly made his business proposal to me.

"You will close all your factories," he said.

I was about to stop him, making sure I'd heard correctly. But he kept talking, not missing a beat.

"You will sell all your equipment," he continued, "and get rid of your people. We will do everything. We will build your furniture for you, more cheaply than you ever could."

Finally, he took a breath and smiled. "You must put yourself in my hands," he said. "You will find our terms highly favorable. I will take care of you."

He went through his prices with me, and I have to say they were staggeringly cheap—so cheap I was certain there had to be some misunderstanding or mistake. Prices this low couldn't cover his material costs, much less labor and overhead.

"You will lose money selling so cheaply," I said.

He nodded. "I understand that. This is the tuition we pay for getting all the business."

I left without giving the factory owner an answer, but I knew I would never agree to anything like that. Close all our factories? Fire all our workers? As I walked out of the factory owner's office, I could already imagine my grandfather turning over in his grave. Contract with this man in northeast China? Place ourselves, our entire business, in his hands? No way! What my Bassett ancestors had spent a century building, we would take apart just like that?

Right then and there I decided: I will go to war first.

THE DEVIL'S BARGAIN

It was a devil's bargain the Chinese factory owners were offering—and not just to us. As I learned quickly, other American furniture makers were getting the same offer, and many of them were saying yes. They would still design the furniture. The Chinese factories would build whatever the Americans specified. The furniture would be floated back to the United States in large sealed metal containers on mammoth cargo ships.

These foreign-produced pieces would still be sold under familiar American brand names—Stanley, Bernhardt, Lexington, Broyhill, or dozens of others. Made in America? Who would know the difference? Most customers would never even think to ask. Many venerable American furniture makers found the deal almost irresistible. Running American factories is a messy, expensive business. Something is always breaking. Someone always needs a gentle reprimand. American workers aren't inexpensive. They want retirement programs and health plans and vacation pay.

Look at the enticing upside of accepting the Chinese deal. The American manufacturers could skip all the headaches and expense of employing real, live human beings in American factories. Within a relatively short time, virtually all our competitors responded the same way:

- They panicked.
- They closed their factories.
- They tossed their people out of work.
- They added another name to the growing list of products that are hardly made in America anymore.

Many of these American factory owners never even paused to consider, "Isn't there some way we can compete here in America? Don't we have some advantages the foreigners don't? Do we really want to walk away from so much knowledge and experience?"

"What choice do we have?" many of my old friends and competitors said to me when I raised an occasional eyebrow over the swiftness of their surrender. Scared they'd be trampled in the rush to the bottom, many of these American companies never even put up a fight. "You don't want to get left behind," they warned me. "The dance card is filling up."

So many of the great names in American furniture making became little more than wholesalers and marketers, sending more and more orders to Asian factories even before the last inbound shipping container emptied out. The Americans would design and decide how much they could sell, but they wouldn't employ a single factory worker or own a single furniture plant.

This wasn't unique to the furniture business. Something similar was happening across many other proud American industries:

- Clothing
- Textiles
- Shoes
- Toys
- Steel
- Household appliances
- Computers
- Televisions
- Small electronics

It half-happened to automobiles, though Detroit bounced back in time to save some of that business from overseas competitors.

Foreign competitors have made big inroads in many other solid American industries—aerospace, agriculture, industrial machinery, the list goes on. In those fields and others, more and more of the American economy keeps drifting overseas. Good luck finding an American-made cell phone or pair of sneakers today!

As our competitors in the furniture business started closing their local factories and America began to lose another slice of its manufacturing base, I felt like our company still had the basic ingredients to succeed right here at home. We had a talented workforce capable of making top-quality furniture. We had an experienced management team that understood the industry intimately. We had access to capital, which I knew would be necessary as we geared up for the future. We had the trust of customers and retailers who'd had good experience with our company and liked the products we made.

That was a lot. And I hated to waste it.

But we also had to recognize that we faced a daunting array of threats. I understood that. We had hard-driving competitors. We had a higher wage structure and stiffer regulation from our government. We had many ancillary costs of doing business. We had consumers who didn't always know—or care—where their furniture was built.

On paper, it was a tough decision. If we had sought guidance from consultants and economists—we didn't—I have strong suspicions what their advice would have been.

Do it.

Close your factories.

Sign on with Mr. Dalian.

Truly, it was touch-and-go for a while.

But not all decisions are made on paper. Paper reveals only so much. I knew in my heart that our company had what it took to make a go of it, and I knew how important that was. We owed it to our company. We owed it to our people. We owed it to our communities. We owed it to America.

All those things mattered to me.

THEY'RE COMING FOR YOU, TOO

We are just one company in just one industry in a diverse national economy at a time of rapid change. We make furniture, that's all. We don't trade stocks. We don't sell burgers. We don't try to be anything we aren't. We build nice-quality bedroom suites that go in people's homes.

But if that's the field we have chosen, I say, "Why not do it right?"

Some folks might look at us and say, "Well, what do you guys know about my business, sitting down there in Virginia with your sawdust and your lacquer guns and your sanding machines?" Everyone's business is different. And every industry is its own little world.

Yes, it is, and yes, it is.

But competition is competition, and you'd better be ready for whatever it throws at you.

The simple fact of the matter is that there are lessons every business leader needs to know. God willing, your industry doesn't face all the challenges ours has. Hopefully, you'll never face a drunken taunt like I did in Hong Kong. But almost certainly you will face competitors at least as dogged and relentless as ours have been.

You don't have to go looking for them. They will almost certainly come and find you.

And when they do, you'd damn well better be ready for them.

THE LEADER'S ACTION PLAN: CHAPTER 2

COMPETITIVE INSTINCTS

DON'T WAIT FOR CHANGE TO OVERTAKE YOU.
See what's coming over the horizon and act as soon as you
grasp what you are up against. Don't hold out for perfect
knowledge or absolute certainty. There is no such thing.
You'll never get anything done that way. Sometimes you
have to go with your instincts.

RECOGNIZE THE VALUE OF WHAT YOU HAVE.
Someone always has something that you don't. We're all at a
disadvantage somehow. But you have powerful advantages,
too. We built a business on the unique talents and overlooked
skills of the American worker, which we possess in
abundance. Great people doing great work close to home.
That's what we had. Figure out what you have, and ride it
hard!

**BE SKEPTICAL OF OFFERS THAT SEEM TOO
GOOD.** When the Chinese factory owner said he'd be happy
to handle all our manufacturing—no hassles, no fuss, and
at rock-bottom prices—I couldn't imagine ever agreeing
to that. I knew it wasn't my businesses he was generously
trying to benefit. It was his! I would not do that to my

people, to my legacy, or to myself. Always ask yourself:
What's in it for us?

BE WILLING TO TAKE A RISK. Every large
achievement entails risk. Failure, perhaps even huge failure,
is always a possibility. Embarrassment could easily be
lurking around the corner. That's inherent in any significant
choice. But with that risk comes the possibility of reward.
Managing the risk is often the only way to get there. Take
smart, calculated risks. Don't be reckless, but have some
guts. That's the pathway to success.

Chapter 3

It Takes a Winning Attitude

Our workers could see the other factories closing. They had friends and relatives being tossed out of work. They worried about their futures. Our people couldn't entirely avoid asking themselves, "You think we might be next?" Defeatism seemed to be just floating around in the air. That's a very dangerous mindset, even when it's partially justified. Whatever people were saying on the street, I knew we couldn't allow ourselves to think like losers, even for a minute. We had to make sure all the dire predictions didn't make us start believing we were doomed. To cultivate a winning attitude in the face of so much negativity, we had to create our own counter-narrative.

Imagine if one of our legendary football coaches were replaced by a Wall Street MBA. I can see it now. The new guy would march into the locker room just before kickoff to deliver his pregame pep talk. "Okay, boys," he'd tell his players. "The oddsmakers in Las Vegas say we are nine-point underdogs. So listen very carefully. Try to lose by no more than eight points."

No! A football coach never talks that way. He only wants to win. Nick Saban, Urban Meyer, Bear Bryant, Bill Parcels—pick your favorite, past or present. He isn't concerned about the odds against him or beating the point spread or eking out a place on someone's nice-try ledger book. High school, college, or the pros, football coaches don't keep their jobs by suggesting that losing is an acceptable outcome. They pull an upset. They outfox their opponents. They take whatever talent they have on the field and will it to victory. That's why I always say: We need more football coaches in this country and fewer MBAs.

I have nothing personal against men and women who further their education in business school. My two sons and my son-in-law all did that, and I love 'em. They all have excellent leadership skills. It's just that too many of today's so-called business experts are so obsessed with their quarterly earnings reports, P&L statements, and quantifiable data points, they tend to lose sight of the crucial human side of any enterprise. They barely notice the awesome power of a winning attitude.

Vince Lombardi, the sainted Green Bay Packers coach whose name is on the trophy that goes to the Super Bowl winners every year, certainly understood that. He loved quoting an expression that was first used by UCLA Bruins coach Red Sanders. "Winning isn't everything—it's the only thing," Vince and Red told thousands of players over the years, 2,122 miles apart.

Let me tell you something I've discovered in my long career: Refusing to accept defeat is at least as important in business as it is in football. It's just a whole lot rarer in the business world, where too many people are glued to all the wrong indicators and make excuses when the results come up short. At Vaughan-Bassett, there were many reasons to skip the fights we entered. Certainly, the odds were against us, even if the bookies never put an official number on it. But I can say this much with certainty: We wouldn't have accomplished anything without a winning attitude.

Companies that have it can overcome daunting challenges. Companies that don't have it can't get out of their own way. They can be loaded with high-priced talent and every advantage in the marketplace. Chances are, their dominance is already starting to fade.

A winning attitude almost never bubbles up on its own. Like underdogs in a locker room, those feelings have to be coaxed, tended, encouraged, and fed. The effort has to start at the top and permeate everything. To win, you have to want to win, know you can win, insist on winning, refuse even to consider the possibility of not winning—and then get out there and bring those victories home.

No disrespect to the importance of watching the company's balance sheet. I do that, too, like a hawk. But a winning attitude has to be at the center of any company's playbook, as it is on every winning football team. Go, Bruins. Go, Packers! Go, Vaughan-Bassett! Win with a winning attitude.

WINNING ATTITUDE 101

There are some practical questions we have to ask:

- What exactly makes up a winning attitude?
- How can it be created inside an organization?
- How can it be cultivated?
- How much difference can attitude really make?

Those are excellent questions. The answer to the last one is what makes the other three worth focusing on, far more than most people realize. It is, quite simply, the difference between success and failure.

The first step in creating a winning attitude is to carry yourself like a winner. Believe you can win! The specific problem that we faced in our business was the sense that everything around us was going to hell and the growing assumption that, chances were, everyone in our struggling industry would end up there eventually. Our workers could see the other factories closing. They had friends and relatives being tossed out of work. They worried about their futures. Our people couldn't entirely avoid asking themselves, "You think we might be next?" Defeatism seemed to be just floating around in the air. That's a very dangerous mindset, even when it's partially justified. Whatever people were saying about us on the street, I knew we couldn't allow ourselves to think like losers, even for a minute. We had to make sure all the dire predictions didn't make us start believing we were doomed.

To cultivate a winning attitude in the face of so much negativity, we had to create our own counter-narrative. Just like one of those top-ranked football coaches and his pregame pep talk, we had to map out our own plan of how we were going to win. I knew a lot of this counter-narrative needed to come from the top. It was crucial, therefore, to lead by example. If Vaughan-Bassett were going to survive, we had to make clear that the owners and managers believed that defeat was unthinkable, period. We were going to survive and thrive. We knew we were. And we were diligent in explaining to our people how we were going to do it, even as we were just figuring it out for ourselves.

In casual conversation and in meetings around the plant, Doug, Wyatt, and I spoke constantly about our commitment to keep the factory open and our belief in the hometown workers we were banking on. We hammered that point, as did the other managers. "We're here to stay," we said over and over to our employees. "Together, we will figure out how to meet our challenges and achieve our goals."

We exhibited exactly the same enthusiasm when we spoke with others in the industry, even when our peers reacted with shaking heads and condescending eye rolls. "You'd better make your deal with one of the Asian factories," they kept warning us.

"We're staying right here," we answered them.

We weren't the only ones who had to embrace that story. We had to make sure our employees did, too, and we had to sell it to the public. Sell it to our competitors. Sell it to the waitresses at the County Line Cafe. Sell it to anyone who would listen and maybe even a few who didn't want to.

Some of our methods might sound almost trivial. They were anything but. I went to Lands' End and ordered a variety of sweaters nicely embroidered with the Vaughan-Bassett logo and presented them to employees who met their sales or production goals. Pretty soon, people were sporting that logo at Horton's Super Market, the bowling alley, and the Galax Plaza shopping center. That symbolism meant something. Without saying a word, people were displaying pride in the company and a belief in our future here. Believe me, others noticed. On more than one occasion we awarded V-B engraved Simon Pearce beer mugs to members of management who came up with effective cost-saving ideas.

These little pride premiums weren't expensive, and we didn't make too big a deal out of them. We had a story to tell, and these small rewards helped to tell it.

Talk alone wasn't enough. I didn't kid myself. I knew it would take more than sweaters and beer mugs to quiet the skeptics. Our employees were still going home at night and hearing all the depressing talk from their relatives and friends: "How are you guys ever going to compete with the Chinese?" they were constantly asked.

In my business and in yours, it has to be words *and* action, plenty of both. That's the second step toward having a winning attitude. Demonstrate by your actions that you mean what you say. In our case, nothing spoke louder or more clearly than the money we spent on the plant and new equipment. People don't think you're planning to close your business when they see you investing major money in it. When we refurbished our plants, people noticed and started saying, "Maybe they really do plan to stick around."

That was a commitment we had to make if we were going to thrive. The plant was antiquated. The equipment was a generation or two behind the times. Our new competitors weren't scared of spending money. Heck, to put us out of business, they were willing to dump foreign-made furniture on the American market beneath their actual cost. These were people you had to confront straight on.

"I don't want to just hold my own against the competition," I told the board when I laid out my plan to invest a lot of money and modernize our factories. "I want to leapfrog 'em." Thankfully, the board agreed this was the time to think big.

Before we were done, we would invest $96 million in new equipment and plant expansion. We would improve our own production techniques, adjust our prices, and create new product lines. The first phase of the plant work was so massive the contractors brought in a helicopter to install giant support beams. We don't get a lot of helicopter traffic in Galax. It's fair to say all that buzzing drew quite the attention around town. "Now they're bringing in helicopters," people were overheard saying between innings at Felts Park.

My point wasn't bravado. I wasn't trying to shock anyone. We were spending money making our operation more efficient because that's how we were going to compete and win. It had been a long time since we or our peers had spent money to renovate on this scale. But we felt like winners, and winners are willing to spend. That attitude helped to save us.

We would deliver the same message by standing up to the Chinese. Taking on a country that was wiping out an American industry was a clear statement that we expected to compete and win. Some people still thought we were crazy or deluded or wildly optimistic, but no one doubted our sincerity anymore. No one would go to all that effort and expense on a lark. Just the amount of time and effort involved made the statement, "We are fighting. We aren't running away." The message was hard to miss. It said: "We are willing to do what it takes—whatever it takes—to defend American manufacturing and to save this business of ours. We are alive. We are fighting. We intend to win."

We were doing whatever it took to succeed. Message delivered, message received.

BELIEVE IN YOURSELF ENOUGH
TO TAKE RISKS

To have a winning attitude, you have to believe in yourself enough to take risks, especially when unexpected challenges arise. Like all other Americans, we were shaken by the terrorist attacks of September 11, 2001. Our management team, our line workers, our vendors, and our customers—how could we not be? Two thousand nine hundred and seventy-seven people were killed that day at the World Trade Center in New York City, in rural Pennsylvania, and just up the road from us in northern Virginia at the Pentagon. It was the worst attack on U.S. soil ever, and the people responsible weren't just targeting our land or our citizens. They were assaulting our entire way of life.

The weeks following 9/11 were an especially dicey time to be running a business in any industry, especially ours. People weren't thinking of going out and buying bedroom furniture. We weren't buying new cars and making any other major purchases. Americans weren't in a mood to spend money on much of anything except the Stars and Stripes.

President George W. Bush fortuitously recognized the economic damage a fearful population could do. He was concerned enough that he made a direct request to all Americans. "Go shopping," he said. "Buy stuff. Keep the economy rolling." It sounded like an odd suggestion at first, standing up to the terrorists by heading out to the mall. Actually, the president was on to something.

The terrorists were trying to intimidate us, economically as well as physically. We could answer by showing we wouldn't be cowed.

At Vaughan-Bassett, we could see immediately how the attacks of 9/11 could threaten our employees, our retailers, and our own bottom line. We knew we couldn't and we wouldn't take that sitting down. The entire culture of our organization was built on the American spirit and refusing to accept defeat, especially when threatened from abroad. Doing nothing was out of the question. We had to react to a threat as profound as this!

Quickly, we came up with an idea. Operation: American Spirit, we called it. We invited every one of our three thousand accounts to participate, from the million-dollar-a-year big boys to the tiny independent dealers who typically sold a couple of thousand dollars of our furniture a month. The deal worked like this: For three months—October, November, and December—anyone who met a predetermined sales target (about 20 percent above the previous year's fourth-quarter sales), would receive a 5 percent rebate on every single Vaughan-Bassett piece that was sold. Four and a half percent of that would be kept by the retailer, an unexpected bonus at a potentially dicey time. The other half percent would be donated to the New York branch of the American Red Cross in the retailer's name.

The program really struck a nerve. Hundreds of our retailers, including most of the big ones, participated in Operation: American Spirit, met the sales targets, and got the rebates. Despite the fear and the experts' warnings, Americans really were out there shopping. They were following the president's advice.

We ended up sending the retailers more than $900,000 and donating $92,000 to the Red Cross. We took out a two-page ad in *Furniture/Today,* our big trade paper, listing the names of all our

American Spirit retailers. And we had a terrific fourth quarter of 2001.

Ours was the only major 9/11 effort in the furniture industry. It produced enormous good feelings all around. To me, it felt like an ideal blend of patriotism, charity, and capitalism—and 100 percent American from beginning to end. Operation: American Spirit worked because it represented who we are and what America is. And thankfully, the broader economy hardly slowed down at all—until the following year.

By then, the national economy really was groaning. Housing sales, the best single indicator of demand for furniture, were way down. The Chinese had started dumping large loads of cheap products on the U.S. market, hoping to suffocate American furniture manufacturing once and for all. Business was slow for us, and it didn't show any signs of perking up anytime soon. Plain and simple, our factory wasn't busy enough. The production line that had been running five days a week was suddenly running four and a half.

When a factory isn't busy, bad vibes abound. It isn't just that new people aren't getting hired or that fewer pieces of furniture are moving off the loading dock. Less money is coming in, and the pressure to cut only intensifies. Should we lay off employees? Should we cut production hours? Neither of those is a happy scenario. You're telling loyal workers, "Don't come in tomorrow"—or you're telling them, "Come in for fewer hours and get paid less." Either way, you're sending a scary message without intending to: Your jobs could be at peril.

Running short time is always a miserable move, even beyond the immediate reduction in pay. With less revenue, there's less to cover the costs of design and planning, less to support training and technology and all the other ingredients that keep a manufacturing business healthy, growing, and strong. And there's one other danger when a factory goes on short time. Almost inevitably, the employees slow down. They may not do it consciously, but they work more slowly. They don't want to finish at eleven o'clock on Friday morning. They want to work until three thirty or four. Somehow or another—and often, it's hard to figure out how—they create enough work to fill the usual forty-hour week. What should take 35 or 36 hours starts taking the usual 40—with no extra furniture to show for it. You end up paying the people for those five or six hours anyway, and you lose money even faster than you were losing it before. It's a vicious cycle.

So what's the answer when times are so tough?

Many experts counsel patience in a take-your-medicine kind of way. "Just wait," they say. "Business is cyclical. It'll improve eventually. Just hunker down and ride out the decline."

Patience certainly has its virtues. Even in a highly successful company, not every year will be a banner year. But when the economy began to stumble in 2002 and things got slow at Vaughan-Bassett, we weren't comfortable just sitting around doing nothing, waiting for improvement. We decided to act assertively.

It was easy to see that people everywhere, including our customers, were struggling. We needed a strategy that took this into account. We set a challenge for ourselves and our employees. Could we build a five-piece bedroom suite that we could sell for $150 less than the least expensive suite currently in our line? This was for the headboard/footboard/rails, the dresser/mirror, and the chest of drawers. Our entry-level set at the time was $750 wholesale. "It'll be worth it even if we have to price it at a small loss," I said. "Hopefully it'll stir things up a little."

We thought hard about our production techniques. We included the employees in all these discussions. They didn't need to have their arms twisted. They were eager to help with anything that might make the factory busier and put them all back to work. We asked questions like, "How much can we speed up the line without losing quality?" "Can we produce a lower-cost item that we can still be proud to put our name on?"

After some intense brainstorming, we came up with a simpler-to-build bedroom suite we could sell for $599. We even had two different styles to choose from. It wasn't quite the equal of our higher-priced products, but the pieces were attractive. The workmanship was solid, and the pricing was unbeatable. My son Doug coined these our Barnburners, which is a hokey name, I admit. We knew the term from watching ACC college basketball. When a really tight game was moving into the second half and the energy in the arena was just about to explode, one of the announcers would often exclaim: "We've got a real barnburner on our hands tonight!"

I'm not sure if people are familiar with that expression in Boston or Chicago or New York City, but everyone in the South knows what a barnburner is. It's something special and exciting. And it precisely captured the feeling we were going for. These $599 bedroom suites were our Barnburners.

Our first test of the Barnburners came at the 2002 Tupelo Furniture Market in Mississippi. Wyatt and I were on a trip to Germany at the time. Doug was at the market. This was back before international cell phone coverage was very good. We had to communicate by fax. This would be a little clumsy, we realized. But it was all we had. Twice a day, we agreed, Doug would call the factory in Galax and inform my assistant, Sheila, how things were going in Tupelo.

Sheila would fax the information to our hotel in Germany, and I would fax back whatever instructions I had.

We were prepared for a good reaction, but I'm not sure we were prepared for this. Even before the show officially opened, word spread around the market how hot these Vaughan-Basset bedroom suites were. The whole place was buzzing. Clearly there was a demand for a lower-priced line that was produced by the Vaughan-Bassett crew.

There was just about a stampede.

While our Mississippi sales rep was inside the showroom meeting with one account, three or four others were outside, banging on the glass and pointing inside. The ones looking in held up two fingers and mouthed the words through the glass: "Two and two," meaning send me two suites of Barnburner I and two suites of Barnburner II. Our rep nodded okay and jotted a note to himself. Only then would the buyers leave. They knew their orders had been recorded.

After the first day it was obvious we were going to sell a lot of Barnburners—at least a thousand Barnburner I suites and another thousand of the Barnburner II suites—during that three-day Tupelo market. Doug reported to Sheila and Sheila faxed it to me. From Germany, I faxed back to Galax: "Put the factories back on full time. We're ready to roll."

CHANGING THE FEELING FUNDAMENTALLY

The risk we took paid off. What on paper looked like a several-hundred-thousand-dollar loss turned out much better than that. Because we were selling so many Barnburner suites, the cuttings got bigger, which helped to lower the unit cost. We initially lost less money on the Barnburners. Then we started making money on them. Those suites also got the factory running faster than ever, which sped up the pace of everything else. *All* the lines got faster. Suddenly we had enough work in the plant to fill up a forty-hour workweek. That sure beat short time! It even meant a little over-time. And people were approaching the regular production with a whole different attitude. Our Barnburner idea just recharged the atmosphere in the factory, lifting everyone's morale.

This was all very different from what might have happened. In a typical factory, when business gets slow, the managers start push-ing their sales reps harder, pushing their accounts harder, pushing their employees harder. The executives ask themselves: "How are we going to generate more business when none seems to be out there?"

We believed the most important thing was keeping the facto-ries busy and the profits flowing from a full factory. It was a very aggressive and a very satisfying one. We just went back and did what General George Patton had advised. "When in doubt, attack," he said. It may not work every time. But what you were doing up to now wasn't working, and at least this shakes things up.

The willingness to take an unconventional approach was part of our winning attitude. Failure wasn't acceptable. Short time wasn't good enough. For our management team, winning was the only tol-erable alternative. It's been a defining principle for us. It's almost impossible to be part of a team with that kind of energy and not be swept up in it.

THE LEADER'S ACTION PLAN: CHAPTER 3

WINNING WAYS

DON'T ACCEPT OTHER PEOPLE'S VIEW OF YOU.
Create and embrace your own narrative. That's what
confident leaders do. At Vaughan-Bassett, if we'd accepted
everyone's downbeat assessment of our industry, we'd be
just another empty brand of generic imports—not a growing
company that stands for something true. Either that or we'd
be out of business entirely. Often those other people know
less than you do.

PUT YOUR MONEY WHERE YOUR PLANS ARE.
You know the clichés: Spend money to make money. Invest
in your future. Put some skin in the game. Those expressions
are true. If you don't believe in yourself and your company,
why should anyone else believe? And talk isn't enough. You
have to prove it. You need, to quote an old cliché, a little skin
in the game.

**SAY IT UNTIL YOU BELIEVE, AND BELIEVE IT
UNTIL IT COMES TRUE.** Your attitude really does affect
your performance, and before you can convince others, you
have to convince yourself. Watch top athletes prepare for a
high-pressure moment. They'll often give themselves a little

talking-to. We all need to do that sometimes. The path is just ahead: Say it. Do it. Succeed.

DON'T HIDE YOUR WINNING ATTITUDE— PROJECT IT EVERY DAY. Attitude is every bit as contagious as the Hong Kong flu. One person can spread a sense of failure through an entire company. That's why I try constantly to project a winning attitude. If I have it, others almost certainly will, too. Good and bad attitudes are equally infectious. Be sure the good one is the stronger of the two.

Chapter 4

Treat Your People Like People

None of us who run businesses are anything without the loyalty of our employees. We need to treat them exactly as we'd like to be treated in return, the old Golden Rule I learned at Pocahontas Baptist Church as a child, the one from the Bible, not the cynical version that snidely says: "He who has the gold makes the rules." Despite the sometimes brutal pressures of competition, we should all try to rise above that kind of cynicism once and for all. Business is a people business, whatever business you are in.

"John?"

I looked up from my cluttered desk to see Shirley standing in front of me. Shirley was an older woman who'd spent several years working in our factory. She was a warm, generous church lady whose husband had died sometime ago. I knew she had a daughter and at least a couple of grandkids.

"Hi, Shirley," I said, motioning to one of the chairs in front of the desk. "Sit down."

It was during an especially rocky time at the height of the rush overseas. Several other local factories had closed already, and things still seemed shaky for us at that point. We had firmly committed to staying in Galax, but there was enormous doubt in the industry about how much longer we'd be able to keep that promise. We were hopeful but not out of the woods, not even close.

"You know, I was thinking about retiring before too much longer," Shirley said.

"I know you've been saying that," I answered.

"I've saved some money," she said.

"That's always good," I said.

"Something's come up," Shirley continued. "My daughter is married to a very nice gentleman. He has a good job, and they have the chance to buy the house of their dreams. The bank is willing to lend them the money, but they're asking me to countersign. It would make me so happy if my daughter and her husband could get the house. They're so excited about it. But John, I have to ask you—am I going to have a job?"

I understood Shirley's apprehension. That same question was on a lot of people's minds. People around town were discussing it, though no one had put it to me quite so directly. And I didn't want to answer carelessly.

"Let me think about it," I said.

I went back to Shirley a couple of days later and told her I'd given some thought to her question. I had an answer for her. "I can't guarantee what will happen to the company," I said, "but I will promise you this: If there are two people left here, you will be one, and I'll be the other."

Shirley didn't miss a beat. "That's good enough for me," she said, before driving over to the bank to sign her daughter's loan.

Now, fast-forward two years. The factory was running and gunning by then, and Shirley was still working with us. Orders were flowing in, and people in the industry were starting to believe we might actually have a chance. But we still had a lot of progress to make. As part of our effort to step up production, we came up with a factory-wide employee raffle. A big one.

"Thunder and Lightning," we called it. There were signs all over the plant: HAVE YOU SEEN THE LIGHTNING? they said. HAVE YOU HEARD THE THUNDER? People really got into it.

The good ol' boys in our area love to hunt. People deer hunt, bird hunt, squirrel hunt, rabbit hunt—any kind of hunting. So we picked up four Browning shotguns. That was the lightning. The second-prize winners would each get one of those Brownings. The top prizes—the thunder—were a pair of brand-new, $20,000 Harley-Davidson motorcycles, one to each of the top two winners.

At the time, there was a twelve-month backlog for those motor-cycles. But I'd been to a conference where the CEO of Harley-Davidson had made a presentation about his company's efforts to revitalize a great American brand. The last thing in his presentation was a photo of a hairy-chested, muscular guy in a brown leather vest. You couldn't see the man's face, though tattooed on his shoulder was a large Harley-Davidson logo.

"How many of *your* customers tattoo your name on their body?" the CEO asked.

I got in touch with the CEO when we were planning our contest. He put me on with a sales manager who arranged for us to acquire two new Harleys without the usual wait.

The day we announced the raffle, we brought the shotguns in, and then a couple of experienced motorcycle riders drove the Har-leys up a ramp and onto the factory floor. They were revving the engines—the roar of thunder!

When things finally quieted down, I explained to the employees that the contest would run for six months. "Every time your team meets the production goal," I said, "your name goes into this big metal bin. When your team meets the safety goal, your name goes in a second time. The same thing every time you have perfect atten-dance for the month. You can get your name in multiple times."

The employees performed beautifully. Many of them reached all their goals. When the final day arrived, the mayor of Galax came to pull the winners' names out of a bin spinning around on a motor. There was real excitement in the air. Everyone wanted to see who was going to win.

Mayor C. M. Mitchell picked the shotgun winners first. Every-one cheered. Then he pulled out the first Harley winner. Cheers were even louder. When he picked the winner of the second Harley, you can probably guess whose name he pulled out.

Shirley's.

Shouting with excitement, she rushed up and stood next to the bike, which looked about twice her size.

People started to cheer as they imagined Shirley riding her new motorcycle. Well, that never happened. She opted to take the cash equivalent of the motorcycle, and that $20,000 was just enough to pay off her part of the daughter's house note.

I couldn't think of a better winner, and I believe most of the employees felt the same way.

It was obvious we all cared about each other in ways that have gotten a lot less common in American business these days.

PEOPLE BEAT NUMBERS ANY DAY

I don't tell Shirley's story just to demonstrate what nice people we have working for us at Vaughan-Bassett, though we do. I tell it because the story perfectly illustrates the culture that pervades our company and makes us who we are. That Shirley would be comfortable having that conversation with the company chairman. That I wouldn't be put off by her openness, even though I had to sleep on her request before answering it. That the other employees would be happy for Shirley and also get a kick out of the idea of her riding a Harley. We at Vaughan-Bassett are people who know and care about each other, not just fellow toilers at a big factory in town. Our company is built on human relationships, and that means treating each other with respect.

As I like to say: Business is a people business, no matter what business you are in.

I know some people say their companies are like a family. To me, that's not the right analogy, though we do care deeply about our employees. But we don't kid ourselves. Vaughan-Bassett is a business, first, foremost, and always. We have a chain of command and a clear hierarchy of authority. Our employees work for pay. If people don't do their jobs, they can get fired. None of that's true in a family. It's difficult to fire your cousin or your children or your parent no matter how they might disappoint you. That's why I speak of our company as a team—a team of mature adults, working together for a shared cause. We admire and appreciate each other's talents. We respect each other enough to be open. We share the good news and the bad. We work together in different roles for a mutual, overriding cause. And none of that can be fully explained as anything but living, human relationships.

None of us who run businesses are anything without the loyalty of our employees. We need to treat them exactly as we'd like to be treated in return, the old Golden Rule I learned at Pocahontas Baptist Church as a child, the one from the Bible, not the cynical version that snidely says: "He who has the gold makes the rules." Despite the sometimes brutal pressures of competition, we should all try to rise above that kind of cynicism once and for all.

Numbers are important, but people matter more. It's a distinction far too few of today's top business executives seem to grasp anymore—to their ultimate detriment, I would add. It's like they all forgot where they came from.

In the financial world, data points get all the attention. People make their fortunes moving money around, not actually creating anything. Hardworking Americans who build real companies with their blood, toil, tears, and sweat are treated like just another entry in the expense column. They are easily and rapidly downsized the minute the market shifts or the margins decline.

It's this approach to business that motivates the hedge-fund and private-equity types who stand ready to swoop in and pile a mountain of debt on a solid company. They say they are extracting unexploited value, wringing out the inefficiencies. Aren't they often risking the company's future and draining the business of its strength? And for their trouble, they pay themselves exorbitant fees and leave the workers to shoulder the burdens and get left holding the bag. I don't believe it's a good practice to take a company with a strong balance sheet and weaken it with a big load of debt where management gets a hell of a payout in three to five years, regardless of how the company performs. That's not business. That's exploitation.

This often trickles down from Wall Street, especially into large corporations and lately into medium and smaller companies as well. Is this practice taught by some of our top business schools? I frequently chastise American business for having this mindset. Businesspeople love to look at figures. Numbers line up quietly in neat little rows, and you can interpret them however you please. Numbers aren't emotional like people are. You don't bump into numbers, all sad-eyed at the grocery store, after you've fired them. People are more complicated. They can sometimes make you feel guilty. They might even talk back. I think that's why businesspeople like numbers so much.

THE BAD-BUSINESS SELF-JUSTIFICATION GLOSSARY

A whole language has grown up to shield executives from the human consequences of the decisions they make. I'm going to teach you how to talk modern business the way these people do.

- "It isn't personal," they say, meaning "we'd like to ignore all the human consequences of the decisions we make."
- "It's just business," meaning "don't be mad at me for firing you or reducing your salary or cutting your health-care benefits."
- "That's the bottom line," meaning "don't waste my time on your concerns. Let me make as much money as quickly as possible, everything else be damned."
- "It's out of my hands," meaning "I don't want to go to the trouble or expend my personal capital to do something that even I know is right."
- "That's above my pay grade," meaning "I'm going to blame others for my inaction even though I could easily act if I wanted to."
- "I'd like to help, but the bankers/the regulators/the board/the lawyers/the accountants won't let me," meaning "I don't have the guts to take responsibility for this decision so I'm blaming everyone else. But I still want you to like me."

I take a far more modern view. Count me as a lifelong capitalist who recognizes he'd be nowhere without his people and therefore believes in always putting them first. They're the ones who make us successful. Whatever the organizational chart may say, it's people who are really in charge. A consultant can tell a factory owner to speed up his production line. But unless the line workers accept the need for faster production, the effort is doomed to fail. A sales manager can lecture his staff about the need for more signed contracts. But unless the sales force feels motivated to sell the product, it will never sell. A team leader at a dot-com can yell till 3 a.m. about the need to pump up the number of unique site views. It'll never happen unless the programmers and the copywriters want it to. We depend on the people we have around us.

These initiatives to favor the numbers over the employees almost always come from the main office, and the main office is almost always far away from the plant, spiritually if not geographically, though usually both. These ideas never float up from the factory floor, where people actually know the ins and outs of manufacturing a product. Many times there's not much incentive to change from the factory floor. At most companies it comes from the outside looking in.

At our company, the main office is physically attached to the factory. I can hear the machines rumble and the fans roar from my desk chair. I can hear them even louder when they stop. Then I'm quickly on my feet going to see what the problem is and how I can help to solve it. I have no desire to relocate our headquarters away from our plant. I often point to the factory and say, "There's where we make the money." Then I point to the office and say, "There's where we spend it." I make sure the factory is well taken care of.

We'd all do better to learn how to encourage, motivate, and reward the people who really make our businesses profitable. Do it because it's the right thing to do. It's in everyone's self-interest. It contributes to the bottom line.

WORKING TOGETHER TO ACHIEVE MUTUAL GOALS

I would never claim that Vaughan-Bassett is the perfect company. I'm not sure there is such a thing. Like any organization, we have our own passing disagreements and personality conflicts. But from the day we opened for business, we have always understood that we must work together to keep this enterprise alive. It really is about the people. And we won't forget that until the day we unplug all the machinery and close our doors for good, which I'm hoping is a very long time from now.

The free clinic is a good example of that. Vaughan-Bassett contracts with a group of physician assistants, overseen by a local medical doctor, to provide free health care to company employees, their spouses, and their children. The clinic is open in the afternoon and evenings to give first- and second-shift employees access to a PA without missing work. It actually saves us money by creating a healthier workforce, but that's not the primary reason we did it. During the financial crisis we had employees dropping their health insurance, and we grew concerned about them and their families. "We've got to do something to help these people," we said. And we did.

Over the years, we have invested millions to increase the efficiency of the equipment in our plants. We've traveled the world reviewing the latest technologies. We've upgraded from three-axis routers to five-axis routers, more efficient machines that move multiple directions. We have cutting-edge machinery and the most modern woodworking factory in the country.

When we buy more efficient equipment, we don't lay people off. The workforce reduces naturally through attrition by not replacing people who leave. Therefore, we don't have people resisting new ideas or new equipment.

The impact of new technology and equipment isn't half as important as what we get from our people. They're the asset that really matters, the one that ultimately determines whether we succeed or fail. So of course, we have to invest in them.

When we closed our Elkin, North Carolina, factory in the darkest days of the 2009 Great Recession, we didn't sell the building or auction off the equipment like most companies would have. We mothballed the plant instead. We haven't started it up again yet, though nothing would please me more than getting those people in Elkin back to work. By maintaining the equipment in the factory and leaving the conveyor lines intact, that's at least a possibility.

The point is: We will spend a hell of a lot of money on what our employees need—decent pay, quality health care, new equipment. We don't spend money on fancy leather chairs for the boardroom or lobby portraits of the handsome executives. Our office décor leans more toward framed desk photos of people's children and grand-children. Our boardroom has had the same chairs and table for the past twenty-five years. None of the upstairs offices, mine included, has a window. Maybe it's a southern trait, I don't know, a sense of community obligation my mother and ministers at Pocahontas Baptist drilled in me. As a young southern boy, treating people decently was inoculated into my upbringing and education. That's just what you do.

People know when you care about them. Employees would rather work for someone they admire, and they will work harder and smarter and longer when they respect their bosses. We've tried—maybe not always successfully, but we've tried—to create that atmosphere, that camaraderie.

These concepts may sound obvious, but in business today, this approach is actually pretty bold. Certainly, few companies take it as seriously as we do. But we never kid ourselves: We would be noth-ing without the people we depend on and serve:

- **Employees**, whose talent and dedication are what all busi-nesses are really selling, whenever the company pops up in the Yellow Pages or a Google search.

- **Customers**, whose affection and choice are translated into the dollars that pay for everything.
- **Vendors, suppliers, shippers, marketers**, and others whose materials and expertise we depend on.
- **Owners and managers**, whose vision and leadership organize the efforts of everyone else.

You notice I put the bosses last. That was intentional, but it's not to suggest that leaders are expendable or interchangeable in the business world. That is most certainly not true. Good leaders are vitally important and the best ones are rare indeed. Without the right leaders—owners and managers both—no company will ever reach its potential. This is as true in a tiny family business as it is in a publicly traded conglomerate with shareholders and employees around the globe.

Every last one of these people craves respect, opportunity, a sense of connection, recognition, and thanks. It's the good leader's challenge to figure out what mix of all that will get the best performance out of everyone in the long run. That's impossible until you step back from the spreadsheets and start listening to people for a change.

So what does this mean in practice? Will we always look to each other for answers to whatever challenges present themselves?

Don't get me wrong. We want to make a profit at Vaughan-Bassett. We *need* to make a profit. We're here to make furniture with our employees and build a successful company, one I hope will thrive for many years. We won't be in business long if our company doesn't make consistent profits over the years. But our ROI, NPV, EBITDA, and all the other ways of measuring success don't mean anything without our human team.

THE LEADER'S ACTION PLAN: CHAPTER 4

R-E-S-P-E-C-T

DON'T TREAT YOUR EMPLOYEES LIKE CHILDREN IF YOU WANT THEM TO ACT LIKE ADULTS. Every parent knows the power of expectation: "Give the kid a name to live up to." Why is that so hard for businesspeople to grasp? Too often, they treat their employees as if they can never be trusted—or are too dumb or lazy to figure out what to do. No wonder there's so much alienation at work. Tell your people the truth. Solicit their input. Set high expectations. Demand that they be met. You'll be surprised how often they are.

REMEMBER THAT YOUR SUCCESS DEPENDS ON THEIR MOTIVATION. So always keep them motivated, employing all the creative ideas you can dream up. At Vaughan-Bassett, we have some of the best employees in the business, but we still have incentive programs, attendance bonuses, and various other feel-good strategies. It keeps the energy pointing upward, and people always like getting something extra.

DON'T ACT LIKE YOU'RE BETTER THAN THE PEOPLE WHO WORK FOR YOU. Everyone shares the same ambitions: supporting their families. Feeling good about their work. Pursuing a set of hopes and opportunities known as "the American dream." Let your people know you get this. They will recognize immediately if you don't. The same way they can tell if you are lying to them or keeping them in the dark about important issues, they can tell if you look down on them. No one works hard for someone who condescends to them.

SHARE THE REWARDS AS WELL AS THE RISKS.

Not every executive is willing to cut his pay or defer his bonus, though far more of them should. But the employees should always be recognized and rewarded when the balance sheets are robust and the times are good. That's only fair. It's also motivating. A year from now—or a week from now—you may be asking them to sacrifice. Let them remember you were generous when you were able to be.

Chapter 5

Totally Transparent Leadership

Our executive pay scale is nowhere near the industrial norm. Just like with the employees, we pay ourselves what the company can afford, which we like to think is less than we're actually worth. I'm not complaining, but neither do we shower ourselves with fancy perks. There's no company plane, no company cars. The company doesn't pay my golf club dues. Our executive suite—I smile when I use a term like that—is a set of half-walled workspaces up a set of stairs from the factory floor. No vast marble lobbies. No expensive art collections. No grand fountains out front. Just an open lot by Chestnut Creek where we and all the employees park our cars, with a few extra spaces for visitors. Ten percent of all of our profits go into the employee profit-sharing plan.

There are many reasons to admire Winston Churchill: his amazing prescience about the growing threat of the Nazis. His steadfast resolve during the darkest days of World War II. His ability to craft a vital alliance between an overwhelmed England and a reluctant United States. But I most admire Britain's wartime prime minister for the way he spoke with utter frankness to the people he was chosen to lead. He never wavered, and he didn't sugarcoat the truth. To be an honorable leader, you must have people's trust. You win that trust, most of all, by telling them the truth.

Churchill became prime minister just prior to the evacuation of Dunkirk. For England, the war was off to an abysmal start. The Nazis were on a rampage across Europe, seeming to gobble up new territory every week. They showed no signs of stopping. Churchill's predecessor, Neville Chamberlain, had pursued a tragic policy of appeasement. The Nazis could be placated, he assured his countrymen, and England would hardly have to suffer at all.

There is always an audience, I have discovered, for what people want to hear. But Churchill knew how dire the threat was, and he refused to pretend otherwise. He stood in the House of Commons on May 13, 1940, after just three days in office, and really laid it on the line. "I have nothing to offer but blood, toil, tears, and sweat," he told the MPs and therefore the entire British population. "We have before us an ordeal of the most grievous kind. We have before us many, many long months of struggle and of suffering."

That was a terrifying message. After all they had been through already, do you think the people of England wanted to hear that? Regardless, Churchill's words were necessary. His assessment was neither encouraging nor optimistic. But it carried the awesome power of transparent truth.

"You ask what our aim is?" he continued. "I can answer in one word: Victory! Victory at all costs! Victory in spite of all terror! Victory, however long and hard the road may be, for without victory there is no survival."

The response was as electrifying in the House of Commons as it was across the Western world. A motion of confidence was promptly and unanimously passed, declaring "the united and inflexible resolve of the nation to prosecute the war with Germany to a victorious conclusion." The British people and their politicians were fully behind the war effort at last. They would remain so until the end.

Churchill's words were so clear on that day, they still pack a punch three-quarters of a century later. Not long ago the Bank of England decided to issue a new five-pound note. The bill features a stern-faced portrait of the man those people still call the British Bulldog and his most immortal words: "I have nothing to offer but blood, toil, tears, and sweat." Well into the twenty-first century, people still rally around that potent truth.

BUILD TRUST BY SHARING THE HARD TRUTHS

In business and in government, building trust is one of the most difficult achievements, but it's hugely important. That's true in any joint human endeavor. If you had a serious illness that could be terminal, you'd want a doctor you trusted. So why would you put your future, your livelihood, or your career in the hands of a businessperson who could not be trusted to tell the truth? I know I wouldn't. So I want to be the leader people can trust.

At the very start of this journey of ours, I made a promise to the people who worked for me. It was just three sentences, but a genuine commitment was packed inside these simple words.

"I will tell you the good news. I will tell you the bad news. But I will never knowingly lie to you."

We weren't facing the threat that Churchill's England was. Bombs weren't falling on Galax, though they might as well have been. Factories were closing. People's jobs were hanging by a thread, as were whole companies, ours included. The stakes were high, and people were watching and waiting to see what we would do. I knew the only way to respond was unblinkingly, as Churchill had. There was no room for weaseling here.

I put the word *knowingly* in there—that I will never *knowingly* lie—because like any human being, I can occasionally be mistaken. And facts do sometimes change over time. Six months from now, I might have to revise my opinion on some issue or reverse a decision I previously made. That said, I have always promised my people that I will never tell them anything less than the honest-to-God truth.

Never. Ever. Ever.

Whatever the issue, I approach it exactly the same way:

- Here are the facts, as I know them.
- Here is my reaction to those facts.
- Tell me your ideas so I can weigh them fully.
- Here is my decision and the reasons behind it.
- And then I implement my decision.

I call this approach totally transparent leadership. I don't hide the important things. My employees appreciate that. I tell them when business is booming. I am just as forthright when business is slow. Do we need extra productivity from the employees? Are we scrambling to stay out of bankruptcy court? Or conversely, are we breaking new productivity records every week? Whatever it is, the circle of trust includes everyone.

When I make a statement, I want people to know they can take it to the bank, write a check on it, and get their money—my word is that solid. Beyond the human decency of telling the truth and the pure joy of constantly saying what's on my mind, I know that, somewhere down the line, I am going to ask these people to do something difficult. And I want them to believe me when I say it's for our mutual good. It could be anything. "We need to work harder." "What we tried isn't succeeding." "We have to come up with a smarter plan." In this competitive world of ours, there's no room to equivocate. So I always tell my employees the truth.

In return for this disclosure, I expect their best efforts every day to help the company succeed. We don't need to be locked in an adversarial relationship, labor versus management. Our interests are aligned. We can operate as people working together for a common goal—to do good work, to produce good products, to save a good company, to preserve good jobs. Everyone gets this. We have a solid base for trusting each other. We share the truth.

When you lead with truth, you treat people with the respect that they deserve. You provide them the tools to react effectively. The organization benefits in the long run. Employees may have ideas that are valuable. If they know and believe in the agenda, they'll work extra hard to help solve whatever problems arise. And really, what's the alternative? People aren't stupid. Chances are, they'll learn the bad news anyway. And if you tell them first, they are far more likely to jump in and help.

Ironically, it's often the hard truths that build the most credibility, exactly the things people would rather not hear. Remember the Jack Nicholson character in the movie *A Few Good Men,* the U.S. Marine colonel standing guard at the wire at Guantánamo Bay, Cuba? "You can't handle the truth!" he famously says in the courtroom. He was right. People can find the truth highly uncomfortable. He was wrong in believing they have to be shielded from its sting.

Because here's what I've learned: People can handle a lot more truth than is commonly imagined, including the really tough stuff. It's when a leader is delivering the difficult news and calling on people to step forward that they most appreciate the transparency. That's when they often come to recognize: This guy isn't just talking. He is giving it to us straight. We can totally believe him—good news, bad news, or in between. If I want people thinking I'm that kind of leader, I have to earn it with my frankness and my transparency.

So why is that attitude not more common across corporate America?

TRUST IS FRAGILE

I have a real problem with the way many of America's top business leaders behave. An unwarranted sense of entitlement coupled with a refusal to reveal the whole truth has crept into the psyche of American business. The higher people rise in the business world, the stronger they seem to feel its destructive tug. They lose touch with their people. This is something all successful leaders must guard against. At the very top, it causes a dullness that will not serve an organization well in the long run.

Special stock for the executives. Royal perks that keep them apart from their own employees. PR staffs and investor relations counselors who do the communicating for them. Golden parachutes when they screw up so badly they need to be dismissed. And the worst part of all this corporate excess is that after a while the bosses start feeling entitled.

At too many companies, the executives are overcompensated for poor results. At Vaughan-Bassett our executive pay scale is nowhere near the industrial norm. Just like with the employees, we pay ourselves what the company can afford, which we like to think is less than we're actually worth. I'm not complaining, but neither do we shower ourselves with fancy perks. There's no company plane, no company cars. The company doesn't pay my golf club dues. Our executive suite—I smile when I use a term like that—is a set of half-walled workspaces up a set of stairs from the factory floor. No vast marble lobbies. No expensive art collections. No grand fountains out front. Just an open lot by Chestnut Creek where we and all the employees park our cars, with a few extra spaces for visitors. Ten percent of all of our profits go into the employee profit-sharing plan.

We don't receive pay raises until our factory employees do, and when times were really lean during the recession of 2008, Doug, Wyatt, and I stepped up. We eliminated our own bonuses and paid the employees'. More than once, we've reduced our own salaries—not because the board of directors forced us to. We just believe the people should get theirs first.

The other day, I was talking with several of our workers in the lunchroom. "When are we getting a wage increase?" one of them asked.

I think he already knew the answer, but he figured—why not ask?

"We don't pay you what we want to pay," I said. "We're paying what we can afford to pay. Nothing would tickle me more than your getting an increase. We want you to get it." I didn't have to finish the rest of the thought. *Help us grow this business. Come up with better ideas. Work harder. Work smarter. We will rise as one.*

He understood that.

He and the other employees are aware that my sons and I and other managers have sacrificed personally just as they have. We are in the trenches with them.

POOR, PITIFUL, WELL-PAID EXECS

I believe in paying talented people for their work, their time, and their ideas. I believe great leaders contribute mightily to a company's success and should be well compensated. I have no problem with any of that. But there is a difference between "well compensated" and the over-the-top pay packages bestowed on many of today's corporate chiefs. How does this look to the employees, who are struggling every day to pay their mortgages and wish to be treated like partners in this cooperative endeavor we call a company?

A recent survey from the Economic Policy Institute of America's 350 largest companies found that the average CEO earned $16.3 million a year, including salary, bonuses and exercised stock options—or 300 times more than the average worker. That number has increased a whopping 997 percent since 1978, even factoring in inflation. During that same period, the typical American worker got a pay raise of—drum roll, please—11 percent.

No wonder executive compensation is being scrutinized. No wonder shareholders are starting to complain. No wonder employees distrust what their bosses say. Too often, the boards of these free-spending companies are cowed by management—or totally out to lunch. They've forgotten a basic tenet of running a productive organization: Everyone has to benefit from the company's success.

So how much is too much? The statistics should make you gasp. At large companies, the typical CEO now pulls in 303 times what the typical full-time worker earns. That's far greater than it was when I was first making my way in the business world. In 1965, the ratio was 20 to 1. I don't remember managers back then feeling unmotivated.

Are we really supposed to believe that today's C-suiters are that much smarter and harder-working than the ones who built America into the most powerful economic force in the world? I wonder how many of today's companies will even be around half a century from now.

In an attempt to shame these executives and wake up their napping boards, the U.S. Securities and Exchange Commission recently required public companies to begin reporting their "pay ratios"— how much the executives make compared to the workers. We'll see who is and who isn't susceptible to shame. But I'm not getting my hopes up. Even the most minor pullbacks in executive compensation are treated like great indignities.

I was invited to a casual dinner not long ago. The guests included several people who held top jobs at one of America's leading banking conglomerates. In the course of the evening, several of them mentioned they were not making quite the same salaries they had before. This was during the Great Recession, and I knew the bank had been struggling.

One woman was especially vocal. She'd been accustomed to earning a solid six-figure salary including bonuses, stock options, and other bennies. She was certain she was worth not a penny less. "I need my salary back," she declared at one point, as if someone had stolen her paycheck out of her mailbox.

"What about your shareholders?" I asked.

"They'll be fine," she said dismissively.

"Their dividends have been cut to almost zero," I reminded her. "The stock price is way down. Some of these investors may be widows and orphans. You're dealing with people's IRAs and pension plans."

"They'll be okay," she said again. "Investors take risks."

I know I should have stopped there.

"Why do you think you're more important than your shareholders? They're the people who own your company, and they're getting nothing back!"

There was an uncomfortable silence at the table. "Well, you have to pay for talent," the woman finally said.

I don't mean to pick on her. Nobody likes a pay cut. She's not alone in feeling dissatisfied. But she was expressing a dangerously out-of-touch method of running an organization. She was implying: I matter, and nobody else does. It's greed, when you get right down to it. It goes back to what the Chinese factory owner told me back in Hong Kong: We have you people figured out. I didn't enjoy hearing that, but part of what he was saying is true.

WASHINGTON, DISTRICT OF CLUELESSNESS

No one is more opaque than a Washington bureaucrat. Politicians are the world's greatest experts at saying whatever it is people want to hear right now—one thing one day, something else the next. They hate to upset people. They want votes so they shade the truth. No wonder so many people are sick and tired of politicians.

Occasionally, a government official speaks up—or tries to—and gives the rest of us hope. In the late 1990s Brooksley Born chaired the Commodity Futures Trading Commission, the federal agency that oversees the futures and commodity options markets. While she was in the job, she pressed Congress and President Bill Clinton to grant the commission greater oversight of the exploding derivatives markets. "We need clarity," she pleaded. These highly speculative investments, she contended, weren't just putting people's funds at risk. They were threatening the stability of the banking system.

Born's warnings were ignored. Her calls for reform were resisted by Federal Reserve chairman Alan Greenspan, Treasury secretary Robert Rubin, and most of the other top federal regulators, along with anyone who was anyone on Wall Street. They all teamed up and let derivatives run wild, keeping Born's skeptical agency away from their latest shiny toy.

You know what happened next. The derivatives market collapsed, costing trillions of dollars. Some of the biggest names in American banking were brought to their knees. The American taxpayers were forced to bail out these gargantuan corporations, who were declared too big to fail. And the nation had to suffer through what became known as the Great Recession, which did a real number on our company and thousands of others across the economy.

A decade later, Brooksley Born was being hailed as a prophet in Washington and on Wall Street by some of the same people who'd given her the cold shoulder before. She even received the John F. Kennedy Profiles in Courage Award for the "political courage she demonstrated in sounding early warnings about conditions that contributed to the current global financial crisis."

Too bad no one listened sooner.

DOING BETTER HERE

At Vaughan-Bassett, I know how much we have benefited from aligning the people and the enterprise. And that always begins with keeping everyone informed.

That transparency and the trust this approach built over time is what enabled our company—employees and management—to pull together and stare down the threat of voracious competitors, Chinese imports, a terrible financial crisis, and whatever else we encountered. That's powerful. Over the years, it has saved us from innumerable catastrophes.

THE LEADER'S ACTION PLAN: CHAPTER 5

NO SECRETS HERE

GET PEOPLE ENGAGED BY LETTING THEM KNOW WHAT'S HAPPENING. You can't expect people to feel loyal to a cause they aren't aware of. They have to know what they are working for, especially when it's time to sacrifice. Knowledge promotes engagement, which promotes commitment, which promotes success. None of that ever happens in the dark.

THEY'LL FIND OUT ANYWAY. People aren't nearly as clueless as you may think. Chances are, whatever's happening inside the company, they're already aware of—or soon they will be. Let your employees hear it first from you. Workplaces are beehives of traded information. People talk. People gossip. People moan and groan. And secrets almost never stay secret forever, even the ones you think are most closely held by management. Let some sunshine in, even some storm clouds if they're on the horizon. It'll be good for everyone. So suck it up. Talk to them. Just don't be surprised when they roll their eyes and say, "Yeah, we knew that already."

TELLING THE TRUTH ISN'T NEARLY AS HARD AS YOU THINK IT IS. Keeping secrets, that's what's difficult. Nothing bad will happen from your transparency, only good things. The employee won't think any less of you for including them in the conversation and soliciting their ideas. They'll respect your openness. They might even say, "Thanks for including us. How about this idea?"

HIDING THE DIFFICULT REALITIES WILL NOT MAKE THEM GO AWAY. If secrecy were really a solution, I'd recommend it wholeheartedly. In fact, secrecy makes almost everything worse. It builds distrust and resentment. It makes people wonder what else they don't know. It deprives you of the input of the greatest experts at your disposal, the people who are already working for you. And whatever the problem is, it's still there—only now it's worse.

Chapter 6

Tough Decisions

Do it? Don't do it? Without a doubt, this was the toughest decision of my life. And it wasn't tough just for me. It could force us all to face some painful questions and literally split our industry in half. Were we furniture manufacturers or furniture importers? Did our brands mean anything? In a modern, global economy, did American manufacturers have a prayer anymore? I'd be dragging all that into the open. Everyone would have to choose what side they were on.

This was going to upset a lot of people. I knew that from the start. If I pushed this anti-dumping investigation, I wouldn't just be accusing a bunch of faceless Chinese factory owners of violating international law. I'd be hurling a lightning bolt through my own beloved industry. These were my colleagues, my competitors, and some of my dearest friends. A case like this would affect American furniture manufacturers large and small, as well as shippers, suppliers, and hundreds of retailers we counted on to sell our Vaughan-Bassett bedroom suites.

Did I really want to take this on?

Many American manufacturers were already getting their furniture made in the very same Chinese factories I was railing against, while they simultaneously ran their own factories back home. What would a fight like this mean for them? Would they still be able to get the low-cost imported products if they stood up publicly against the Chinese?

This issue put retailers in an awkward position as well. Most of them were selling the lower-cost merchandise from abroad. Whether they were passing the savings on to their customers or pocketing some of the profits for themselves, they were benefiting from the cheap imports. Would they still be able to buy from Chinese sources if they were also claiming it was illegally subsidized? This uncertainty gave the retailers reason to feel defensive.

But what about American factory workers—our own employees and the tens of thousands of others who toiled in our industry? What was our obligation to them? Was it fair for them to lose their jobs because of illegal trade practices on the other side of the world? Shouldn't our people get a level playing field and a fair chance to win? These were all excruciating questions—and universal ones.

Do it? Don't do it? Without a doubt, this was the toughest decision of my life. And it wasn't tough just for me. It could force us all to face some painful questions and literally split our industry in half. Were we furniture manufacturers or furniture importers? Did our brands mean anything? In a modern, global economy, did American manufacturers have a prayer anymore? I'd be dragging all that into the open. Everyone would have to choose what side they were on. Yes, this was business, but it was also personal. The toughest decisions almost always are. And no one had any idea how this one would turn out.

DECISION TIME

There is no easy way to make a hard decision. You have to

- Gather as much information as possible.
- Figure out what it all means.
- Balance the conflicting obligations.
- Take inspiration from the wisest people you know.
- Make the hard choice yourself.
- Recognize you'll never please everyone.

There were plenty of conflicting obligations in deciding to proceed with the anti-dumping petition. I had an obligation to the company I led. I was responsible for guiding it toward success. I had an obligation to the industry that had nourished us for decades. I had an obligation to the people who worked for me and an obligation to the communities we all called home.

We didn't have to take on this fight. I realized that from the start. My sons and I could have gone to High Poin, opened an office, and become importers like everyone else was doing at the time. My sons and I discussed this explicitly: "What if we joined this import bandwagon? We'd have no shortage of company. What would be the most efficient way for us to do that?"

There's no doubt we could have followed that path. With an assistant, an office manager, a personal computer, and a cell phone, we could have been open for business that afternoon.

We knew how to hire designers and develop a line. We had the industry relationships. We knew the customer base. We had the marketing experience. We could have sourced all our products offshore. That guy in China was offering to build anything we asked him to— at below material cost. "Put yourself in my hands," he told me. "I will take care of everything." If we didn't want to deal with him, there were dozens of others just like him, ready to offer similar deals.

Of course, that would have meant liquidating the company, the machinery, and the plant, which would have earned us only pennies on the dollar, nothing more. There was an awful lot of used furniture-manufacturing equipment on the market at the time. Bailing out would also have meant disposing of the inventory. Those prices started around a 50 percent discount and went down from there. We would have collected what we could from account receivables. You never get 100 percent there. The town would have lost a major employer, and employees would have lost their jobs. And the stockholders' investment would have taken a huge beating, as would their trust in us.

We didn't do that—none of it. We just weren't comfortable throwing our shareholders, our employees, and our community to the wolves. We didn't care how many people were doing it or what a thousand consultants said. Closing the factory would have meant thinking only of ourselves. That's not who we were. We were stewards of this company, and we were determined to make it succeed.

If we'd given up and just become importers, there also wouldn't have been an anti-dumping petition or all the payments U.S. furniture companies received on account of the cheating Chinese. Our shareholders wouldn't have gotten the benefit of any of that. For that and a hundred other reasons, I am certain we made the right choice.

I also had a heartfelt duty that was harder to define—a duty to the family legacy that was handed to me, a century of Bassetts and all they had left behind. I could still hear the echo of my mother's wisdom reminding me, "To whom much is given, much is expected in return."

As I approached this difficult decision—leap in or stay out— hers wasn't the only inspiration I took. Winston Churchill was also guiding me. I often found myself referring to him and trying to decipher how he would approach these decisions.

By early June 1940, the great wartime prime minister realized France was going to fall. America and Russia hadn't yet joined the war. The United Kingdom was in it alone. Churchill knew Adolf Hitler would probably offer England a separate peace: You keep your island, we'll take everything else. Churchill stood tall and said no. He said it with such confidence and bravado, his very words changed the dynamic on the ground. He stood in the House of Commons and literally saved Western democracy that day.

"Even though large tracts of Europe and many old and famous States have fallen or may fall into the grip of the Gestapo and all the odious apparatus of Nazi rule, we shall not flag or fail," Churchill declared. "We shall go on to the end. We shall fight in France.

We shall fight on the seas and oceans. We shall fight with growing confidence and growing strength in the air. We shall defend our island, whatever the cost may be. We shall fight on the beaches. We shall fight on the landing grounds. We shall fight in the fields and in the streets. We shall fight in the hills. We shall never surrender, and if—which I do not for a moment believe—this island or a large part of it were subjugated and starving, then our Empire beyond the seas, armed and guarded by the British Fleet, would carry on the struggle until, in God's good time, the New World, with all its power and might, steps forth to the rescue and the liberation of the old."

By the time he got to "the liberation of the old," there was nobody on that island who did not understand exactly where Churchill's government stood. England was not giving up. Not giving up. Not giving up! Her people would fight—if they had to, forever. Now, those were tough decisions! I wasn't sure I could match Churchill's boldness. My stakes certainly were not as high as his. But he definitely gave me something to aspire to.

Once I'd gathered the facts, weighed my conflicting obligations, and asked what Churchill would do, it all seemed much clearer to me. We were furniture *makers,* not furniture *deliverymen.* With American workers, we produced quality products that represented honest value and improved people's lives. That still meant something in America. I hoped so, anyway. I couldn't betray the people who worked for me or the company that we built together or the legacy that my ancestors had entrusted to me. I knew what I had to do. Fighting this fight, even with little encouragement, was absolutely the right thing. We might save some jobs. We might save this factory, this company, this industry, this town—we might save them all as the proud institutions they deserve to be.

When I looked at myself in the mirror and asked, "What's the right thing to do here?" the answer came screaming back at me.

"Much is expected."

"Never surrender."

"We shall fight."

FREE TRADE, FAIR TRADE—WHY NOT BOTH?

Really, what choice did I have? By 2002, our industry was already sliding into ruins. An important piece of the American economy was being lost. Too many American furniture factories were closing. Too many American workers were on the street. Too many products once made in America were being thrown together overseas, then shipped back here in containers. Vietnam, Malaysia, Indonesia, India—they weren't quite as large a factor yet. The action at this point was mostly in mainland China. The numbers clearly backed me up. In just two years, wood-furniture imports from China were up 75 percent, from $1.65 billion in 2000 to $2.89 billion in 2002. (In 1992, it had been only $129 million, the U.S. Census Bureau said.) In two and a half years, more than 34,000 American furniture workers had lost their jobs. In one survey, 18 furniture makers reported their operating income was down 47 percent. How much longer should we wait?

Let me be clear: There is nothing inherently illegal—potentially tragic but not illegal—about importing goods from far-off countries and selling them cheaply in the United States. Free trade, this is called. But I had the strong suspicion that what the Chinese were doing with their bedroom furniture was something far more nefarious. To me, it smelled like a case of illegal dumping.

This has nothing to do with toxic waste dumps or leaving garbage by the side of the road. "Dumping" is the term lawyers and economists use to describe manufacturers' exporting a product to another country at a price below what they charged in their home market or below the actual cost of production, in an effort to gain market share. Under international law, dumping is considered "predatory pricing" and is clearly illegal. The World Trade Organization condemns dumping whenever it causes or threatens "material injury" to a domestic industry where the goods are being sold.

To supporters of free trade—count me as one of them—dumping is a dangerous form of protectionism. To labor advocates, it's a dire threat to dedicated employees. Economists say dumping undermines the whole concept of fair trade. All I know is it's damn hard to compete with a foreign factory if their government is subsidizing their prices and dumping their products in America at substantially less than the manufacturing cost. That didn't sound fair to me.

Wasn't it exactly what that shady Chinese government official had told me in Dalian when he said he'd be happy to make our furniture for us at ridiculously low prices—as long as we closed all our factories down? "Put yourself in my hands," he'd urged with a smile. His below-cost prices were the "tuition" the Chinese would pay to push us out of the market once and for all. Now he and his colleagues had even larger ambitions.

As far as I was concerned, that wasn't competition. It was somewhere between bribery and extortion, and I wasn't about to give in without a fight. Clearly, these people didn't care one bit about dislocated American workers or wrecked American communities. They were intent on doing whatever it took to wrestle this business from us—fair or not, legal or not, consequences be damned. These Chi-

nese communists, I was discovering, were far more ruthless capitalists than American capitalists ever were.

Now, all we had to do was create a leadership team, gather support inside the industry, convince the federal government that the
Chinese had been playing dirty, and get Washington to act. How
hard could that be?

A GREAT TEAM CAN DO GREAT THINGS

A strong inner circle was key. I knew there was no way I could
lead this effort alone. The group I assembled ended up doing
a superhuman amount of work and achieving extraordinary results.
Thankfully, recruiting them wasn't hard at all. I didn't have to look
far. All of them worked a few feet from me.

I cannot write another word until I single out six people who
were there for everything.

My son Wyatt focused on the legal aspects of the case. With the
International Trade Commission, the Commerce Department, and
Customs involved, the regulations and procedures were hugely complicated. Wyatt became an expert in all of it. You can't imagine how
many wrinkles there are in the federal anti-dumping law. Thankfully,
our industry association, the American Home Furnishings Alliance,
hired the law firm King & Spalding to help us understand what our
rights were and then to pursue them. International trade specialists
Joseph Dorn, Michael Taylor, and Stephen Jones really knew their
stuff. But when the lawyer had an idea, Wyatt would often say, "Wait
a minute, what if we try it this other way?" Often, the attorneys
would agree. He was constantly coming up with fresh approaches.
Anti-dumping standards, sunset provisions, injured parties—phrases
like those just seemed to tumble off Wyatt's tongue.

My son Doug focused on the politics—and believe me, there was no shortage of politics all over this case. As a former Capitol Hill staffer and a lifelong political junkie, Doug has extraordinary knowledge about the inner workings of Washington. Whenever some new issue arose, he got us in to see key senators and congressmen and make the lawmakers actually pay attention. Congressman John Dingle from Michigan, Senator John Warner from Virginia—whoever it was, Doug seemed to have a way in. The politicians didn't always do what we hoped they would. But more often than not, once we explained how we were trying to save a proud American industry and thousands of American jobs, the Washington power players came around. The three of us—Watt, Doug, and I—made many trips to Capitol Hill.

In a case like this, you have to prove everything—how each American company was injured, to what extent, what difference the foreign dumping made. All of it has to be presented in a precise, specific way. A truly endless array of forms had to be filled out. Joyce Phillips, our office manager, took prime responsibility for finding old figures and long-forgotten financial reports. She couldn't have done this without Andy Williamson, our chief financial officer, and Doug Brannock, our vice president of corporate affairs. They had an objective understanding of exactly what our company had been through and knew which data supported the assertions we were making. They had produced many of those reports, so they knew what was in them. Believe me, there were pages and pages and even more pages to absorb. The team's depth of expertise—not just on Vaughan-Bassett but on the furniture industry—was surprising even to me.

Tying it all together, overseeing everything, never missing deadlines, keeping records of every meeting, and handling a thousand other vital tasks was our executive assistant/vice president Sheila Key. Sheila also had the never-ending duty of keeping me organized. That, in itself, is a full-time job.

And my job? I was the leader. I was the mouthpiece. I was the figurehead. Use whatever term you want, I was the one ultimately responsible for making sure our anti-dumping campaign succeeded. Someone had to be in charge, and I was the one. I assembled the inner circle. I kept everyone focused and productive. I dealt with the crisis of the moment—there was always something. I put together the industry coalition. I made the calls and chaired the meetings. I leaned on people to pay their dues and gave pep talks to keep them on board. I took a lot of the flak. When our supporters sometimes got wobbly, I talked them down off the ledge.

All this took a huge amount of effort, but the seven of us— Wyatt, Doug, Andy, Joyce, Doug, Sheila, and I—were the core. It took an enormous amount of time and effort, all while we still had a factory to operate and a company to run. But we were an effective team. Everyone had a job. Every role mattered. We communicated constantly. We had a winning attitude. We didn't panic. I had this team behind me that was irreplaceable, and they were watching my back.

We stuck at it. We never gave up. And inside our industry, we developed some wonderful *allies.*

JUST FOLLOW THE LAW

After his initial review, Joe Dorn and his colleagues at King & Spalding reported back that our complaints appeared legitimate. "There is a strong case to be made that China is illegally dumping bedroom furniture into the U.S. market," he said. But for

the Commerce Department to proceed, we would have to cross that
51 percent "red line." If we did, Joe added, this would be the largest anti-dumping case ever brought by the United States government against the Chinese. They could be forced to pay hefty import
duties—"immediately leveling the playing field."

But it was my job, not Joe's, to get the industry majority on
board. Furniture makers, like a lot of other businesspeople, are an
independent lot, not the kind of folks who go running up to Washington every time they have a grievance. Mostly furniture people just want Washington to leave them alone. Most people in our
industry didn't even know anti-dumping laws existed. In our factories we have to inform employees of their rights to a workplace free
from discrimination on account of gender, religion, race, age, and
other factors. We're required to advise them of their right to a safe
workplace. Yet our own United States Department of Commerce
had never apprised us of our fair trade rights.

As I got busy making the argument to my competitors and my
friends, the media immediately took notice, inside and outside the
industry. "We aren't asking the government for special assistance or
handouts, but to enforce the law," I said to Powell Slaughter at *Fur-
niture/Today,* the trade magazine everyone in our industry reads
voraciously. "We believe in three things: free trade, fair trade, and
legal trade." And lately, I added, we hadn't been getting any of them.

I explained why what we were doing wasn't protectionism. That
was a term our opponents were frequently throwing around. We
were simply asking the federal government to enforce existing U.S.
law and the rules of the World Trade Organization.

"What we are dealing with is a closed economy where the government subsidizes its industry and pegs its currency," I told the *Los
Angeles Times.* The current situation, I said, gives importers with no

domestic plants an unfair advantage. "If you were an importer you would love to compete in America, because we just roll over and play dead."

We got a welcome, early boost from Jerry Epperson, one of the sharpest analysts in our industry. He told *Furniture/Today* our committee had "done its homework and has its ducks in a row." Added Jerry: "I think you'll see more companies join this effort once they're sure it's going forward."

We started with a group of fourteen companies and formed the American Furniture Manufacturers Committee for Legal Trade. We filed the initial petition in October 2003. Along with Vaughan-Bassett, our initial team included some of the oldest names in the business: Hooker Furniture, Vaughan Furniture, The Bassett Furniture Industries, Keller Manufacturing, and L. & J. G. Stickley.

While we gathered support, our early moves also stirred up some staunch opposition. As one old colleague warned me quite pointedly: "You're not opening a can of worms here—you're opening a barrel full. You be careful what you wish for, John."

Our opponents put on a massive publicity campaign, designed to capitalize on the fears of some members of the industry. If we succeeded, the naysayers warned, wood bedroom furniture imported from China would get drastically more expensive, cutting sharply into the profits of the furniture companies that were bringing it here.

This message had some resonance. More and more companies were contracting with Chinese plants. There was a growing hopelessness in the air. Even inside our own company, some people who loved us as individuals didn't seem to think we had much of a chance. "We're just one company and not the biggest," more than one person said. "You really think you can pull this off?" They'd been watching factories close all around and our own production output decline. I hate to say this, but some of them had basically given up.

DUTY BOUND TO SPEAK UP

In January 2004, we won our first victory. The International Trade Commission found "reasonable indication"—the legal term—that less-than-fair-value imports from China were harming the American furniture industry. That was huge. But to proceed further, we still had to get across that difficult "red line."

People were lining up quickly on both sides of it. Some supported us. Some opposed us. Some joined reluctantly, only after we promised we wouldn't publicize their names. It was a hard call for everyone. Ethan Allen remained neutral, unable to make a decision. Furniture Brands, the large conglomerate that includes Thomasville, Lane, Broyhill, Henredon, and Drexel, adamantly opposed us. I knew they were already contracting with Chinese plants. Ashley, the national manufacturer and retailer, also said no way. They were importing heavily from China. La-Z-Boy Inc. and Stanley Furniture made tough choices to support us even though they were also importing Chinese furniture to blend with their own production and enhance their domestic product lines.

The uproar hit its crescendo at the High Point Market in April 2004. Our opponents were working the crowds aggressively, throwing everything they had at us. To make their point, they passed out campaign buttons that featured a picture of a sad-eyed Bassett hound (get it?) and a bold headline that read: HOW BIG IS YOUR DUTY?

The Furniture Retailers of America took out a two-page ad in the April 1 edition of *Furniture/Today* on behalf of the Bombay

Company, City Furniture, Crate & Barrel, JCPenney, Rooms-to-Go, and "more than 40 other small, medium, and large furniture retailers representing approximately 3,400 outlets and more than 200,000 associates." I don't believe it was meant as an April Fools' joke.

"Starting June 17," the ad copy declared, "your bedroom could be subject to a variety of massive import duties. Why are these companies asking to put their hands in your customers' pockets?"

The ad portrayed our petition as futile and counterproductive, damaging to the very industry it purported to save. "These companies surely know that most (if not all) of these bedrooms will never be made in the USA," the ad said. "If these companies win, we all lose."

By that time, we had added ten more companies to our group and lost a couple. The ad named them all. American Drew, American of Martinsville, The Bassett Furniture Industries, Carolina Furniture Works, Century Furniture, Copeland Furniture, Crawford Furniture, Crescent Manufacturing, Harden Furniture, Hart Furniture, Higdon Furniture, L & J. G. Stickley, Lea Industries, Michels-Pilliod Company, MJ Wood Products, Mobel Furniture, Moosehead Manufacturing, Pennsylvania House, Sandberg Furniture, Stanley Furniture, Vaughan Furniture, Vaughan-Bassett Furniture, Vermont-Tubbs, and Webb Furniture. By listing all our names, I guess they were trying to shame us—or threaten us. Maybe both. To me, the message was clear: Don't expect to sell any of your furniture through our stores.

The ad also pounded us with a series of pointed questions, some half-true, some one-quarter true, some hardly true at all:

"ASK WHY the petitioners are seeking duties on Chinese products when a number of them helped set up the Chinese factories that make these products?" Some companies did help, but they never counted on being cheated by the very factories they worked with. That was a violation of trust.

"ASK WHETHER they are seeking dollars only because many of them no longer serve as middlemen earning spreads of up to 40 percent on sales to U.S. retailers." No, we want to build furniture, save jobs, and defend American manufacturing against cheaters.

"ASK WHETHER they filed the petition just to keep the duties for themselves (a recent U.S. law gives them that right)." No, we did it to save an industry and its people, including ourselves.

"ASK WHERE their bedrooms that were previously produced in China are now being made?" In Vietnam, Indonesia, India, and other countries. And if they're violating foreign-trade laws, they should be cited, too.

"ASK HOW much bedroom prices will increase when the duties kick in?" However much the Chinese are cheating, that's what the duties should be.

We had answers to all those questions and many others that ultimately got asked. The more people learned, the better off we would be. All week long I met with industry members, making my case with everyone. I walked the floor. I had breakfasts, lunches, and dinners. I talked to people in all corners of the industry, trying to enlist their support. I held an off-site meeting in Greensboro, North Carolina, for industry suppliers—lumber, hardware, and chemical companies. Their businesses were threatened as well, and I wanted to get as many of them to join us as possible. A couple of companies who were already exporting lumber to the Chinese agreed to help surreptitiously. Others agreed to come right out in the open. We were making headway, but feelings were extremely raw.

I'll tell you how tense the High Point Market was that year. When it was over, I realized I hadn't seen our biggest retailer in

Kansas City, Missouri, a great furniture man and a fine customer of ours. That was strange. He and his team came to market every year. I called to make sure everything was okay.

"Market wasn't the same without you," I said, when I got him on the phone. "Everything all right?"

"John," he said, "we were there. We were just afraid other people would see us going into your showroom."

I was slightly taken aback, but I told him I understood.

"Can you come out to Kansas City and see me?" he asked. "I'd like to have a look at your line."

"Sure," I said. "Happy to." And he placed a nice order when I did.

THE GOOD GUYS WIN

When the vote was finally tallied, we had our 51 percent. We crossed the Commerce Department's "red line." Actually, we did better than that. Fifty-seven percent of the bedroom furniture industry had backed our anti-dumping agenda—not quite a landslide but a solid majority nonetheless. As an industry, we said no to the foreign cheaters. We refused to sit by quietly. We did what we could to protect our companies and our people. And we asked the federal government to enforce the law.

The decision had been hard, but I made it and so had the others.

When the investigation was over, the International Trade Commission ruled with us. On December 10, 2004, the commission found unanimously, 6 to 0, that China had sold beds, dressers, nightstands, and related bedroom furniture "at less than fair value" and thereby "materially injured" American furniture makers. The evidence showed that the Chinese action had the effect of unfairly skewing the competitive marketplace for these goods. It was a text-book case of illegal dumping.

The government's determination was exactly what we had claimed. The largest anti-dumping case ever brought against the Chinese had unequivocally succeeded.

The following month, the Commerce Department imposed duties on Chinese exporters. The tariffs ranged from less than 1 percent to more than 200 percent of the import value.

Did the duties help?

They certainly stemmed the Chinese imports. In 2004, before tariffs were applied, China exported $1.2 billion worth of bedroom furniture to the United States. By 2010, that figure fell to just $691 million. But bedroom furniture imports from Vietnam shot up in the same period from $151 million to $931 million. No import duties are levied on Vietnamese furniture, and workers there earn $80 a month, even less than the $170 a month paid in China. There's no chance of an anti-dumping order against Vietnam because we could no longer garner 51 percent standing in the industry.

By 2009, worldwide imports accounted for 78 percent of the $3.4 billion of wooden bedroom furniture sold in the United States, up from 44 percent in 2001. A few years later the *Washington Post* asked me to look back. Was it worth it, the reporter wanted to know.

"There would be nobody here today if we had not done this," I told him over the din of the factory machinery downstairs, and that was the truth.

"We turned a stampede. No, we didn't bring it to a screeching halt, but we turned it a bit, and we slowed it down."

Winning was nice. So was leveling the playing field a little. So was partly righting a wrong. And beyond all that, the anti-dumping case has helped our industry financially. We certainly needed it.

The penalties have meant significant payments to American furniture makers, more than $300 million over the past twelve years. Not a cent of that money has come from American taxpayers. It came from extra import duties Chinese companies were forced to pay after they were caught cheating. It's how they've had to compensate their dumping victims.

The U.S. Commerce Department determined which of the Chinese companies had been dumping and how high their duties should be. One company from China might pay a 5 percent duty. Another might pay 40 percent—or no duty at all. Companies that refused to cooperate with the U.S. government were socked with a 200-plus percent duty before they could bring their goods into the United States. The Commerce Department also determined how the compensation should be split among American manufacturers, based on what percentage of the market they commanded when the proven dumping occurred.

Now when the Chinese furniture comes in, the U.S. Customs Department collects the duties from the "importer of record." That money goes into a pot for distribution, and the U.S. Treasury Department ultimately sends out the checks.

The mechanics of this keep getting more complicated. In 2007, Congress repealed part of the anti-dumping law having to do with payments to individual U.S. companies. The more recent duties are now paid to the U.S. Treasury, though American companies are still getting payments based on earlier calculations.

The foreign factories keep on humming, maybe harder and faster than ever before. But we are still making furniture in Galax, and everything we did has made America more competitive, not less. Whenever I speak before a business group, someone in the audience will inevitably ask me whether I am a protectionist, trying to put up barriers to the free flow of products around the world. Nothing could be further from the truth. I don't like anyone interfering with free trade. I just want to make sure the trade is legal and fair. In fact, the United States is not especially quick to bring anti-dumping complaints to the World Trade Organization. The U.S. has imposed fewer anti-dumping penalties against other nations than either China or India has. How do I know this? I know it from the WTO's own website. In the 12 years after we filed our complaint against China, from 2003 to 2014, India imposed 315 confirmed anti-dumping complaints. China imposed 161. The United States imposed 149. I'm sorry, but facts are facts. They've been pursuing international dumpers more aggressively than we have. When I quote those figures, that usually quiets the protectionist claims. You tell me who the true protectionists are!

THE LEADER'S ACTION PLAN: CHAPTER 6

TOUGH STUFF

PROBLEMS RARELY DISAPPEAR ON THEIR OWN.
Sometimes, it happens. Sometimes, lightning strikes and
leaves the front hedges perfectly trimmed, though far more
often it burns the house down. The same is true with tough
decisions. Don't hide from them. Face them. Even if your
best decision isn't perfect, chances are it'll be a whole lot
better than doing nothing at all. And if left unattended, most
real problems tend to get worse.

DON'T GET TRAPPED IN THE ECHO CHAMBER.
It's easy to find people who agree with you, especially if you
are paying their salaries. Yes-men and yes-women will nod
along passively until the day the business collapses, then
they'll tell all their friends, "I tried to warn him." Surround
yourself with smart, frank people instead. You'll not
appreciate their every nugget of insight and advice. But even
if you disagree or dismiss what they're saying, just hearing it
will broaden how you think.

BE READY TO UPSET SOME FRIENDS. When we
pursued the anti-dumping petition against China, we
knew not everyone in our industry would be charmed. We
expected some of our competitors to be deeply skeptical,

and they were. After all, our approach cast a negative light on theirs. Colleagues, neighbors, even some family members found ways to let their discomfort be known. Eventually, I'm happy to say, most of them came around, along with a majority of the furniture industry. Even some of the staunchest holdouts reluctantly conceded, "You were probably right." Thanks for that.

ALWAYS INSIST ON FAIRNESS. Most businesspeople aren't quick to complain to Washington—or to anyone else. But this really isn't about complaining. It's about establishing an environment for success. No one should have to compete against cheaters. No one should have to fight a battle that can't be won. But when the competition is a fair one, behold what happens: No success is out of your reach.

Chapter 7

The Change Imperative

Everywhere you look, the business landscape is littered with the carcasses of once-successful companies that hid from, misjudged, or stubbornly ignored the pressing need to change. The world changed. They didn't. Goodbye. Their names were the stuff of legend. They exemplified the power of the U.S. economy. Their employees and investors believed wholeheartedly in them. Even now, their legacies live on. Sadly, their businesses do not. They are gone—or all but gone. Hanging on by threads, these once-mighty companies are now only faint shadows of themselves. I'll bet you still remember most of them.

Have you read *Who Moved My Cheese?*

I'm a big fan of Spencer Johnson's classic business parable about four little creatures living together in a maze. It's a perennial at business conferences around the world. Some executives even assign the book to their supervisors, hoping it will help them do a better job managing change. I've used the book as a training tool, though I have my own twist on what the tale means.

Sniff and Scurry are mice, just a couple of dumb rodents. Hem and Haw are little people-beings who are as small as mice but look and act more like humans. The four creatures have found a corner in a maze, where they are living contentedly, certain they will have all the cheese they could ever need or want. Then one day they notice the cheese is all gone. As you might imagine from their names, each has a different reaction to that. Hem refuses to recognize that anything has changed. The cheese is coming back, he tells the others. No adjustments necessary. Wrong! Haw, who's also slow to act, eventually takes baby steps to find more cheese, has modest success, and is emboldened to keep looking. Sniff, who's been tracking the cheese supply all along, anticipated the decline and is ready to respond to it. Scurry, always quick to act, bolts off in search of a new cheese supply. Each one has a different strategy for dealing with the change.

"Which one is right?" I ask my supervisors after everyone has absorbed the story. "Who should our company be?"

Our people know not to choose the creature who hides from change. They all choose one of the other three and explain their reasons why.

"Those are all good answers," I say finally, "but I don't think any of those is the very best answer."

Puzzled, the supervisors wait for me to explain, wondering what I'm driving at. "You mean we ought to hide from change and just wait for the old days to return?" someone inevitably asks.

"Of course not," I say. "I have something else in mind." Then, I explain. "All four of these options are asking us to decide how we should react when the world changes around us. Maybe that's not the right question to ask. Instead, maybe we should be asking, 'How can we cause the change? Why don't *we* move the cheese? Why not create the change and make *other* people react to *us*?'"

The author didn't have a little creature to represent that option, but maybe he should have.

When the Asian Invasion, as I like to call it, hit us in the furniture business, the Chinese had moved the cheese on us. Many domestic furniture makers, like Hem and Haw and Scurry and Sniff, were unsure of how to react. They all went in different directions. We needed a plan. But instead of running off half-cocked or hiding our heads in the sand or being resentful of the change that was thrust upon us, we moved the cheese on the Chinese. We directly challenged their illegal conduct by bringing the largest illegal dumping petition that country had ever faced—and convinced the U.S. government our claims were correct.

We also stepped up our own game:

- We increased the number of pieces we produced per hour by 25 percent.

- We made our factory more efficient and more profitable.
- We created "Thunder and Lightning."
- We launched the anti-dumping petition.
- We found creative ways to reduce absenteeism and motivate our sales staff.
- We sent people on cruises (without the boss).
- We built a heathier workforce by promoting our health clinic and conducting health fairs.

We made the changes and let others decide how to respond.

Change isn't always easy. Change is not without risk. But let me tell you one thing: It's a whole lot more fun—and potentially a whole lot more profitable—than sniffing around after somebody else's missing cheese. As those mice and their mini-friends learned so vividly, managing someone else's change is no fun at all. That leaves your future in other people's hands. That's why I like our approach so much better.

The Chinese didn't like it very much, as I recall, nor did many of our competitors. A lot of people thought what we were doing was reckless or hopeless or counterproductive or a colossal waste of time. I expected a wide range of reactions, and that's exactly what we got.

Our employees certainly noticed. Willie Greene was one of our plant safety coordinators. He is now the vice mayor of Galax. But when we were expanding the plant, Willie pulled me aside one day.

"John," he said, "may I tell you something?"

"Anything, Willie," I said. "What's on your mind?"

Willie got right to it. "There are people in this town who think you're crazy," he said. All the other furniture companies were doing little or nothing at all. We were jumping into expansion mode.

I thought for a second about how I should answer Willie. Maybe all those people were right. But I didn't think so, and I don't think Willie did, either.

"Willie," I said, "five years from now, come back and tell me how crazy I am."

Willie didn't have to. He got on board from the start.

Move your own damn cheese!

YOU HAVE TO DRIVE THE CHANGE

My father used to say, "Getting on top in business is tough. Staying on top is tougher." He should know. He got there. And he spent decades holding on. Once you start doing well, there is a tendency to say, "Here I am. This is perfect. Let's just stop the world right where it is."

I see this every day—people who quit changing once they achieve a certain level of success. I understand exactly where they're coming from. They don't want to risk what they have in hand. Change can be unnerving. Change asks you to do things you aren't used to doing. You can never be certain how well you or your organization will perform. You may be judged harshly. You might make mistakes. The change you think will help you can turn out to be a bust.

I once saw a revealing survey that said seven out of ten people assert they are in favor of change—as long as someone else is doing it. Unfortunately, life seldom works that way. That answer completely misunderstands the nature of change. If somebody else changes and it is to your benefit, that's terrific. Be grateful. But don't count on it. That won't happen often, and it will almost never happen when you most need it. You'll never stay on top for long waiting around for other people to make changes that benefit you. More likely, your competitors are already eying you, maybe even scheming to topple you from your elevated perch.

Given the pressures of modern business, doing the same old thing just isn't enough anymore. Slavish repetition may be comforting, but it will never sustain you in the long run—no matter how effectively it got you there in the first place. It'll stop you from improving. It'll give your competitors time to copy you, undermine you, and gain on you. You'll get bored and sloppy because all you're doing is repeating what you've always done. Where's the creativity in that? To stay on top, you have to change. You'll probably have to change more than you ever changed before. And you—yes, you—must be the one driving the change.

That's what leaders do. They drive change. They lead their people to keep changing and offer guidance as the change occurs.

Business is a fluid thing. Many times in our business careers, we will end up somewhere far different from where we started and far from where we expected to be. But as we travel that road, we have to keep improving how we and our companies perform. We discover new talents and abilities. We dream up new approaches. We find new segments of the market to explore. And chances are none of that will happen unless we focus on driving change.

When you get right down to it, change isn't just something you do. Change is a mindset, a constant openness to doing things differently than the way they have always been done before. Change is something you approach every day ready to implement. And that takes commitment. You may be required to:

- Spend money.
- Make unexpected alliances.

- Expand the kinds of products you produce and/or services you deliver.
- Find fresh approaches to motivating employees.
- Go after new segments of the market.
- Ask yourself, "How can we do things better?"
- Engage with customers in unexpected ways.

And all those requirements are not guaranteed to succeed! That was another pearl of my late father's wisdom. "If everything you do in business is a success," he liked to say, "then you are probably aiming too low." You aren't taking on large enough challenges. Your ambitions aren't high enough. If everything is an easy success for you, your goals are too short. It's like outrunning a four-year-old. Yes, you won—but how good should that really make you feel? You're running the wrong race. You're not out there on the edge.

Now, you don't want *a lot* of failures. That can be dangerous and not conducive to long-term success. But you should expect some disappointments and occasional failures. Those disappointments will usually indicate what needs to be improved.

Despite my natural competitiveness, I have learned that when my people try things that don't work out so well, I should not be too quick to criticize. Instead I like to recognize that they tried. I say, "Guys, let's keep trying. Let's try not to make the same mistakes, but don't ever stop trying."

You never can tell. A year or two later, something may come up that makes me say: "You remember how we cut this part...or how we marketed that piece...how we handled this other issue in the business? That thing that failed?"

It's like a light turning on.

"Yes," they'll answer.

"You think that might work here?"

Suddenly, that failed attempt from the past now looks more like a wise investment in ourselves that just took a little while to pay off. That is the mindset that will promote creativity and propel change.

This critique isn't a matter of looking for trouble or constantly tinkering or refusing to leave well enough alone. It isn't about panicking in the face of others' fears. I'm certainly not urging change for the sake of changing or because you lack a long-term commitment to your own ideas. You have to change because the circumstances around us are constantly changing, and you have to stay ahead of your own decline.

WORDS NEVER SPOKEN

In my fifty-plus years in the furniture business, there are two things that have never happened to me. I have never had a foreman in my factory tell me he had too many people working for him, and I have never had a salesperson tell me he was outsold.

Never happened. Not once. Not to me.

Factory supervisors always want more people. They need a couple of extra bodies for the finishing line. They want three more people somewhere else. Never once have I had a supervisor or foreman come up to me and say: "I have too many people working for me. Can you cut us back a little? We could get this job done just as well with a smaller crew." In half a century, that's never happened once to me, and I'm not expecting it to happen.

Over the same long period, no salesman of mine has ever been outsold.

I have heard all kinds of reasons why we didn't make the sale. "The price is too high . . . The delivery is too slow . . . The dresser isn't wide enough . . . The chair is too high . . . The finish is wrong . . . We only have three beds. We need five beds." No one ever says, "Our product is terrific, and the service is great. The guys from Broyhill just outsold me."

This refusal to accept unwelcome truths is unfortunate and sometimes damaging. We all have shortcomings. We should work on them, not duck them. If you don't recognize your shortcomings, how can you possibly correct them? If everything you do is perfect, there is no reason for you ever to improve. Perfection is rarely the case. It's not the full story, anyway.

When we first faced the threat of globalization, we hadn't been doing everything right. Our industry was too cozy. We hadn't been pushed to innovate. We had the idea that nothing could really hurt us. Some of us hadn't invested enough. But it wasn't easy getting people in our industry to stop and acknowledge: "Yes, we did some things wrong." This made it all that much harder for people to stay and fight. To survive, they *had to* improve. If you don't look at yourself critically, aren't you destined to make the same mistakes all over again?

After a football game, win or lose, the coach and the players look at the films. They ask, "Why did we fumble on the six-yard line? You see where the quarterback got sacked? Look at what the left tackle did."

If we don't face our failures, we are not driving change. If our competitors are changing and we aren't, we will be the ones falling behind.

IT'S BRUTAL OUT THERE

I've been around the furniture business for so long now people sometimes say I have sawdust running through my veins. But with my long view, I know this much without a speck of doubt: People in business have to keep changing, no matter what. Then, they have to change again. Ask your people to:

- Dream bigger.
- Aim higher.
- Perform beyond what they think they are capable of.
- Expect management to stand firmly behind them.

You have to help them and lead them. Just don't be alarmed at the results. And when things are finally just the way you want them, it's time to change again!

Companies that don't change die. It's that simple and that sad. I used to think this was the special burden of highly competitive manufacturing businesses like ours, racked by globalization, economic uncertainty, new technology, and other unique challenges. Now I see that openness to change is an imperative in almost every field.

Everywhere you look, the business landscape is littered with the carcasses of once-successful companies that hid from, misjudged, or stubbornly ignored the pressing need to change.

The world changed. They didn't. Goodbye.

Their names were the stuff of legend. They exemplified the power of the U.S. economy. Their employees and investors believed wholeheartedly in them. Even now, their legacies live on. Sadly, their businesses do not. They are gone—or all but gone. Hanging on by threads, these once-mighty companies are now only faint shadows of themselves. I'll bet you still remember most of them.

Compaq. E. F. Hutton. RCA. Paine Webber. Eastern Air Lines. Enron. F. W. Woolworth. Radio Shack. Pan Am. Levitz Furniture.

Heilig-Meyers. Arthur Andersen. General Foods. TWA. Lionel Corporation. Adelphia. Bear Stearns. Montgomery Ward. American Motors. Blockbuster Video. Circuit City. Borders. The list goes on.

We've had our share—more than our share—of disappearing acts in the bedroom furniture business. Over the past decade or so, dozens of once-successful case-goods companies have filed for bankruptcy, liquidated their stock, or watched their values collapse in some other unfortunate way. Yes, it's brutal out there.

Furniture Brands, a company with a host of venerable brands including Thomasville, Lane, Broyhill, Henredon, and Drexel, went bankrupt and is now owned by a private-equity firm, their stockholders receiving little in return. Many companies liquidated and disappeared, among them Mobel, Sumter Cabinet, Keller Manufacturing, Cochran, Moosehead, Richardson Brothers, Statton, Athens, Virginia House, and Webb Furniture. Their shareholders took major write-downs. Then there are the companies that continue to operate but don't actually make the bedroom furniture they label and sell. That includes Lexington, Hooker, Bassett, Stanley, Kincaid, and others. Their case-goods factories are closed and their line workers are gone. Many of the once-thriving American communities they supported are now almost ghost towns. There's an emptiness where factory trucks once rumbled across wooden floors, machines hummed, and sawdust flew. There's very little left in communities like Lenoir and Lexington in North Carolina and Martinsville, Pulaski, and Galax in Virginia. Not long ago, I could count nearly one hundred case-goods plants our size or larger, most of which have now disappeared. In our town of Galax, about eighteen hundred people once worked in one of six furniture plants. Now it's only about six hundred. Vaughan-Bassett closed plants in Sumter, South Carolina (V-B/Williams, 300 jobs), and Atkins, Virginia

(Virginia House, 250 jobs). As I mentioned earlier, we mothballed a factory in Elkin, North Carolina (350 jobs). Henry County, Virginia, one of the more devastated communities, had many more furniture jobs than we did. Now they have very few.

All this makes people ask: Can't America make anything anymore?

Maybe a few sheets and towels. A little apparel. Hardly any electronics or personal computers or phones. We lost much of the automobile industry, though give Detroit credit. Before that industry was totally gone, U.S. automakers sprang back. Next on the hit list? An even wider range of industrial machinery and products. Overseas factories started with the simplest products and have moved up the manufacturing food chain. What would make anyone think this all stops with bath towels and bedroom suites? It hasn't, and it won't. Fortunately, some companies have found a way to successfully blend an import model and a retail operation.

You can't only blame the savvy overseas manufacturers. Little of this could happen without the involvement of foreign governments. China today is a crazy blend of communism and capitalism, as are other countries in that part of the world. They pay low wages and pollute their environment. If they need a Keystone pipeline, they don't have a big, angry, climate-change debate. They just build the pipeline. The answer isn't for us to be like them. That's not who we are as Americans. But our companies do have to compete in the world. We have to insist our competitors play by the rules. And if recent history is any guide, we have to be ready for a knock-down, drag-out death match.

We'll be in for more of the same if we lose.

CHANGE, LUCK, AND RESULTS

In the midst of our struggle against offshore manufacturing, I came across a figure that seemed daunting at first. For the cost of every U.S. worker, the Chinese could have 33 workers on a factory line. If you thought about that for long, you could get depressed. I knew I had to find another way to view the comparison, and here's what I came up with. It's from the flip side of the same equation, and it's actually legitimate. When we save 10 people's jobs through efficiency, they will have to save 330 to match us. That gave us some hope and a springboard to act from.

American business will never win a race to the bottom on the wages we pay. Our wages will never be our strongest suit competitively. America is going to have higher wages than a lot of Asian and South American countries do. Instead, our folks have to be smarter, faster, and more productive. That always requires change. We have to exploit the advantages we have, not cry over the ones we lack. If we are going to successfully compete with these nations, we need to have the most efficient operations in the world. That's an advantage we can achieve. We have to maximize it just as we have to take advantage of our proximity to the customer. Our products don't take as long to arrive. For many of our retailers and customers, that's a very big deal. It's an advantage we can use in our fight to win.

At Vaughan-Bassett our goal has never been to slash the payroll, but to grow sales and keep the existing number of people employed with more productivity. We have never gotten rid of one person because of efficiency, replacing a person with a machine. We tell our employees this and we've lived by it: "Don't fight change and efficiency. Your job is not on the line. If we need to reduce the workforce, we will do it through attrition." That commitment and willingness to change walk hand in hand. But it doesn't begin and end with the CEO or the president. Everyone has to be on board. And if business comes to a grinding halt and we have to cut production at some point, reducing the head count might be the prudent thing to do. Such action should always be handled with sensitivity and responsibility to our people.

When someone tells me, "John, no one has ever done this before," or "This can't be done," I am instantly motivated. I want to blaze a trail. In America we have to think that way, now and forever. I never want to make change sound easy or certain or obvious or guaranteed. It's none of those. Even the greatest business leaders can't always maneuver their companies to easy success. Some forces really are greater than a company of smart, dedicated, hardworking individuals. No matter how creative we are, we can't always turn back the tide. Success is never certain, no matter what you do.

That said, don't you have to try? Sure, you do!

In our case, we took a huge riverboat gamble. Hanging tough in America wasn't a no-brainer for us. It was a gutsy decision that could have failed. We didn't have all the answers. We were shooting in the dark to some extent, but we never allowed ourselves to get lost in some grand scheme. We weren't operating in a vacuum. No business ever does. Things change around us even as we change our own paths. The important thing is, don't wait to see how those outside changes play out before starting your own. And when circumstances start to affect what you're doing, respond to the facts as they present themselves.

The economy was getting tougher? We tightened our belts. The competitors fled? We stayed put. The Chinese improved? We improved, too! When we didn't have the luxury of a detailed road map to guide us, we had core values:

- Make a quality product.
- Stay close to home.
- Treat people fairly.
- Be transparent with employees, customers, and everyone else.
- Remain loyal to those who got us here.
- Stay in it for the long haul.
- Remain open to change.

We never knew exactly what changes would be flying at us. We faced the world with an openness to change and an understanding that life in business is also inevitably a leap of faith. We knew who we were. We were willing to make some improvements and take some chances. Thankfully, we have been nicely rewarded for that.

Most of business is common sense. When you get too far from the basics, you lose your sense of direction and start having trouble bringing your people along. If you don't fully understand where you're going, they certainly won't and you'll suddenly find yourself traveling alone. Business is much easier when you have other people traveling with you.

Before my grandfather died, at age ninety-eight, I asked him how he'd managed to accomplish so much in his career. "You can't know everything," he told me. "But what you don't know, you surround yourself with people who do."

I've tried never to forget that. It's not that complicated if you have reliable people who can help.

WHY US?

Given all that was stacked against us, there probably shouldn't be any furniture plants left in the United States. And if one was going to survive, it probably shouldn't have been ours. There were other companies with deeper pockets, richer owners, and larger labor forces than Vaughan-Bassett's. But they didn't have what we had. We had a plan. We had leadership. And we had the will to keep making furniture in America, even as many of our competitors, one by one, went chasing easy profits overseas. We had something else they didn't—unity of purpose. Labor, management, office staff, suppliers—we all had skin in the game. We were all in this together—the workers, the owners, the community, all committed to doing whatever it took to stand tall against foreign competition and keep our American factory alive. Never, ever underestimate the power that American industry and American workers hold in their hands when everyone is pushing in the same direction toward a common goal. And the stakes for us were enormous. We weren't fighting just to save a business or make a certain financial return. We were defending something far larger than dollar signs. We were fighting for the power of Americans to make something valuable, a long-standing legacy of ours that was under attack from abroad. Yes, we needed to make a profit. Yes, the company had to grow. Yes, we had to provide our customers with a better product at a fairer price in a swifter time. Against all odds, all that came together, and we now basically stand alone. With the right leadership, that's an effort people can readily get behind.

THE LEADER'S ACTION PLAN: CHAPTER 7

CHANGE THIS!

IF THE OLD WAY ISN'T WORKING, DOING THINGS THE OLD WAY WILL NEVER PRODUCE NEW RESULTS. Traditions are important. Knowledge is built over time. But stubbornly clinging to past practices will guarantee only one result: You'll live in the past while the world moves on. There's just one test for any business strategy: Is it working for us? If it isn't, ditch it now. Change keeps things interesting. It keeps people energized, fresh, and motivated. Change!

CHANGE OR DIE IS MORE THAN A SLOGAN—IT'S A CONSTANT REALITY FOR EVERYONE. Remember the dinosaurs—*T. rex* and TWA? They once roamed the earth with confidence. Then they crashed down to it. They refused to change, and now they are gone. Don't be a dinosaur. Change. The consequences of not changing are far more dire than you may believe.

ANTICIPATE CHANGE WHILE THINGS ARE STILL GOING WELL. Don't wait for crisis time. It's easy to become complacent. Arrogance is a natural outgrowth of success. Both are traps for the businesses that are doing well. History teaches a difficult lesson over and over again:

Nothing succeeds forever. Tough times will come. Plan for them. That's not looking for trouble. It's being prepared.

DEFINE THE TERMS OF YOUR CHANGE. Don't let others do that for you. Change isn't a multiple-choice test handed down from above you. You get to frame the issue and decide how to respond. You study the options. You rank them as you see fit. You direct the timing, the intensity, and the focus of the change. Others will offer their opinions. They always do. But change is your narrative to define. This is only fair. You're the one who has to live with it.

Chapter 8

Don't Panic

Thankfully, most of us have brains. When we use them, they work pretty well! When we take the time to think things through and judge with insight and experience, we usually reach a reasonable conclusion. It's panic that clouds our thinking and makes us do things that aren't real smart sometimes. Calm reflection won't guarantee that all your decisions will be wise ones. But the odds are far better than with decisions made in panic. Isn't that obvious?!

There's an old southern expression that people still sometimes use. It comes from the days of moonlight and magnolias and carefully choreographed debutante balls and was thrown around quite a bit during the Asian factory stampede.

"The dance card is filling up," our competitors kept warning us, meaning *move your manufacturing to China now or it will surely be too late.*

This was always said in a tone of friendliness, as if our company's long-term well-being were their only concern. Actually, the warning had one purpose and one purpose only: to scare the living crap out of us!

Some of our competitors were preparing to padlock their own American factories and make deals with the Chinese. A few of them seemed a little nervous that we weren't rushing down the same path.

"John," they kept saying, "the dance card is filling up. The good Chinese factories are getting close to capacity. You'd better make your deal soon. You don't want to be left out."

"Thanks for the advice," I'd answer. "But I think we'll be staying right where we are."

Oh, they didn't like hearing me say that!

Panic loves company just as surely as misery does. That's something I've come to notice over the years. When businesspeople are in a panic, they much prefer everyone around them to be panicking, too. Every time they notice someone else in a similar situation who's not panicking—remaining calm, weighing the options, or choosing an alternate path—it feels almost like a personal affront. The panickers start to worry: "What does he know that we don't?" "What's her secret plan?" "Why aren't they running scared like we are?" That can be terribly unnerving. There is comfort in numbers.

So what does a confident leader do? Not panic! Keep your wits about you. Do what you already know to do.

- Take a breath.
- Methodically gather facts.
- Analyze the situation at your pace and on your terms.
- Don't be rattled by complaints or opposition.
- Ask yourself, "Do I really have to act this very minute?"
- Don't judge yourself by what other people think.

That last one, not being overly concerned about the opinions of others, can be highly liberating at a time like this. It's really just a matter of having confidence in yourself. You have to make judgments your way. Without self-confidence, you will always be at the whim of popular opinion—the lowest common denominator of the people you encounter—and you know how often that can be wrong! If you let others spook you, you'll never be any smarter than the people you're competing against. Why give them that power over you? That's somewhere you don't want to be.

Most often, there's no need to panic. Things are rarely as dire and urgent as they seem, despite the breathless warnings of the panickers. And even if the whole world is going to hell, joining in the panic won't do you much good. It'll only make things worse. You'll be responding in a poor emotional state on an unrealistic timetable to other people's exaggerated fears. What's the chance that those conditions will produce good decisions? Panic leaves no room for your own common sense.

A sound business decision is seldom made while people are panicking. Reactions are more effective when cooler heads prevail. I don't suggest you put your head in the sand and refuse to face the facts. Some American furniture factories probably needed to close, and those were gut-wrenching decisions. But there's a difference between moving with alacrity and responding to panic. As gloomy as a situation can appear, don't react until you've cleared your head and thought about what to do. Otherwise, you'll likely regret whatever you do.

Thankfully, most of us have brains. When we use them, they work pretty well. When we take the time to think things through and judge with insight and experience, we usually reach a reasonable conclusion. It's panic that clouds our thinking and makes us do things that aren't real smart sometimes.

Calm reflection won't guarantee that all our decisions will be wise ones. But the odds are far better than with decisions made in panic. Isn't that obvious?

THE STEADY HUM OF COMPLAINTS

People will complain.

Whatever style you operate with, whatever decisions you make, some people won't like it. There is simply no way to please everyone. That's true in any organization. Do not overreact to that. Do not let it panic you. Like many lessons about leadership, I learned that one in the army.

When I was a young second lieutenant with the Fourteenth Armored Cav in Germany, I had a platoon sergeant whose name was Olsen. I never knew his first name, He was just Sergeant Olsen to me. He had been in World War II and in Korea and had hash marks running up and down his sleeves. He also had wisdom about army life that I did not yet possess.

I'd been hearing quite a bit of grumbling from some of the enlisted men in my platoon. Not major stuff, but there was a fair amount of it. The barracks were uncomfortable. No one liked the food or waking up at 5:30 a.m. The supply clerk wasn't responding quickly enough. The men could always find something to complain about. If they weren't drinking beer, chasing girls, or something, they'd fill every silence with low-level complaints.

I asked Sergeant Olsen if I could speak with him. "Let's get a cup of coffee," he said.

Over cups of standard-issue army sludge, I explained that I was worried about the attitude of some of my men. "These guys," I told the sergeant, "they never seem happy, no matter what."

Sergeant Olsen gave me one of his I've-been-there looks. "Lieutenant," he said to me, "I gotta explain something to you. The army is built on bitchin'. You're not gonna stop it. Let me tell you about bitchin'. A certain amount of bitching is just talk. As long as it stays in that zone, we're doing just fine."

I nodded but did not speak.

"Now," Sergeant Olsen went on, "you don't want too much of it. What you also don't want is no bitchin' at all. That lets you know immediately that something is going to happen, and it won't be good."

"So how much is too much?" I asked Sergeant Olsen. "How do you know?"

"That's what you got me for," he said. "I will tell you when the bitching gets too high or when we don't hear anything and need to worry. You gotta understand that's the way the army works."

Eventually, I developed my own ear for complaints inside the platoon. I had a pretty good instinct, it turned out, for knowing the difference between routine grumbling and serious issues that needed to be attended to at once. And I also learned that Sergeant Olsen's bitch line didn't apply only to military life. People in every workplace, every social club, maybe even every family, are prone to a certain amount of complaining. That's just human nature. Don't expect it to change. People aren't going to tell you how great you are all the time. Complaining is a normal part of business. Get used to it. Don't panic. Just be aware when the complaining reaches a certain level—too high or, especially, too low.

THE LANGUAGE OF PANIC

No one will ever come right out and tell you to panic. But people have many ways of trying to provoke panic, pushing others to act on the emotion of fear. Often they do it with code words. I don't hear that "dance card" expression much anymore. Most young people wouldn't have a clue what that means. But here are some other phrases to listen for, all designed to stir panic in your head.

- "People will think you don't know what you're doing."
- "Prices are rising soon."
- "I wouldn't wait much longer if I were you."
- "Everybody else is doing it."
- "You'll be sorry if you miss out."
- "Don't get left behind."

- "New regulations are coming."
- "This could be your last chance."
- "Others will have theirs, and you won't have any."
- "It's already getting hard to find."
- "You saw what happened to those other people."
- "This won't look good."
- "You'll have a lot of explaining to do."
- "This could be your biggest mistake."
- "It'll all be your fault, and everyone will know."

Can't you already feel the anxiety? Just hearing these phrases reminds me how infectious panic can be. However you hear it, the effect is always the same—to rattle your confidence. To provoke hasty decisions. To make you jump when jumping is the last thing you should do. The panickers will warn about some irreversible error you are committing if you persist down your independent path. That is the essence of panic. And this is, too: delivering the fearful message in the guise of heartfelt concern. Be highly suspicious of such overtures.

In the furniture industry, we faced that pressure many times over the years. Close the factories! Fire the workers! Withdraw the anti-dumping petition! Dump the stock! I hate to ascribe selfish motives to other people. It's always impossible to know what's in someone else's mind. But even if their concern is utterly genuine—to help a clueless colleague—the anxiety that stirs up has the same effect: to drag you into their panic.

As it turned out for us, we really could continue making furniture here. We just had to be focused, hardworking, and smart. We didn't panic, and the results speak for themselves. Other manufacturers also made the right decisions. Each must be determined on an individual basis.

WHAT PRICE PANIC?

Panic has many triggers. In our industry, price is one of the strongest. There are few things that raise the anxiety of a businessperson more quickly than picking up the rumor, "A competitor is undercutting our price."

Suddenly, it's panic time!

Actually, businesspeople are susceptible to looking at whatever their competitors have and feeling at a disadvantage, if not completely left out. There is always that tendency. It is especially fierce with comparisons over price. In business, you hear talk like this all the time: "They're selling it for—*what*? How's that even possible? They're gonna kill us now!"

Price panic was one of the factors that drove our competitors to abandon their American factories. Price was the argument the Chinese used to squeeze into the marketplace. "You need to close your plants and buy from us," the Asian factory owners promised. "We can make the furniture cheaper than you can." And many Americans folded without a second thought. Before you knew it, they were throwing their hands in the air and waving the white flag of surrender. They gave up without even trying to win.

But let's face it, price isn't everything. Like many things in life, it just depends.

When we have buying decisions to make, plenty of people, myself included, will want to buy whatever's cheapest. That's understandable, depending on what the product is. When I need to fill my car with gasoline, I may drive to the station across the street if their gas is a penny cheaper. But gas is a commodity. The Shell gas isn't much different from the Exxon gas. All we judge on is price.

Furniture is not a commodity. Manufacturer to manufacturer, no two pieces are the same. When a customer chooses a bed or a dresser, certainly price is one consideration, an important one. But it's not the only thing. If people made decisions based only on price, everyone's bookcases would be boards on cinder blocks. We'd all store our sweaters in cardboard boxes picked up from the dumpster outside a liquor store. They're cheaper than cheap—they're free! But fashion, design, service, quality, how quickly the product can be delivered—all those factors go into someone's decision about what to buy and where to buy it.

It's not just furniture. When I go to a restaurant, I don't always order the cheapest item on the menu. Sometimes I feel like filet mignon or the rack of lamb. When I buy a car, I want good value, but not necessarily a beat-up, secondhand Yugo. And I'm not alone in how I choose a car. When I look out on the road, I see a lot of cars that weren't the cheapest ones on the lot. Watch women and their fashion choices. If a dress does not flatter, a lady will not buy it, no matter how great a bargain it is. Even men, who aren't always quite as fashion conscious as some women, will often pay a few extra dollars to look sharp in a pair of blue jeans. Not everybody buys jeans at Wal-Mart, even though the prices are really good.

People do not buy entirely based on price. Understanding that is a key part of beating back price-driven panic. When the other guy is cheaper, you have to keep asking yourself: "What other advantages do *we* have?"

Our salespeople understand this. It's just that sometimes they forget, and I have to remind them: "What can we do that others can't? Price isn't everything."

LEAD WITH YOUR STRENGTHS

No company has everything, and part of avoiding panic involves recognizing that.

In baseball, there is only one all-star game every year. The best players in the American League take on the best players in the National League—the best pitchers, best catchers, best first basemen, best outfielders, best shortstops and so on. Those are two amazing teams! Then, as soon as the all-star game is over, the celebrated players all go back to their respective teams. Guess what! Those teams don't all have the very best players at every position. Each team has some really good ones and some not so good. No team has a full roster of all-stars. And still, somebody is going to win the World Series that year, just like someone in hockey is going to win the Stanley Cup and someone in football is going to win the Super Bowl, so-so players and all.

Winning is a mindset, just like losing is. You have to shake off your limitations and your assorted reasons for panic—and all of us have some—then set your mind to win.

My favorite word to hate in business is *can't*. It's often a response to panic. When people say they can't do something, that means they've quit trying and they've quit thinking—one or the other, sometimes both. Of course they can't if that's how they think! Talking yourself out of victory, this is called. It walks hand in hand with panic. It is an everyday danger in every successful organization.

To combat this defeatist thinking, you have to find what makes you extraordinary and capitalize on it. At Vaughan-Bassett, we deliver goods faster than anybody else in the bedroom business. The Chinese are good at what they do, but they still have to float that product across the Pacific Ocean. You've heard of "the slow boat to China"? Well, the boat *from* China is every bit as slow. It's the truth! Focused as they are, they are not going to suck the water out of that ocean. The Chinese are not super-people, as I constantly remind our folks.

Salespeople naturally want the finest of everything—the finest designs, the finest finishes, the finest drawers, the swiftest delivery, the best workmanship. It goes on and on. If you bring three of the five, they will say, "Bring me the other two." If you bring seven of ten, they want to know what happened to the other three.

A salesman and old friend of mine once told me: "This is why you have salespeople. If you have the finest of everything, you don't need a salesman. You could send a dog with a note in his mouth. Anybody can sell something if it has absolutely the finest of everything."

This is no argument against high standards. In our company, we are constantly pushing for the highest. But absence of across-the-board perfection can become an excuse for panicking in the face of challenges. We have to get over that.

- Use your head.
- Use your imagination.
- Inspire your people.
- Don't get spooked.

KEEP THE FEAR TO YOURSELF

A nd if you do notice your confidence fading, please, just keep it to yourself.

I tell our managers: "Don't ever let them see fear in your eyes. If they see fear in your eyes, they will have fear in their hearts." Let them look at you and feel assured: You can get the job done and you know it. That's the American way.

Churchill never showed any fear whatsoever. Neither did John Kennedy when he refused to blink during the Cuban Missile Crisis. The Navy SEALs on Team Six didn't blanch when one of their helicopters crashed as they arrived at the compound where Osama bin Laden was hiding. The SEALs pressed ahead and got the job done.

I'll tell you the one who showed fear. President Jimmy Carter, when he spoke of a "malaise" in this country and said it in a way that made people doubt there was any way out. It's hard to know exactly how he felt, but he spoke like a leader who didn't quite believe in the country he was leading. Compare him to Ronald Reagan, who never had a doubt about himself or his country, at least not one he let on about. What did George Washington go through during the Revolutionary War? How did Abraham Lincoln press on when the whole country was being torn apart? They gave no quarter. They showed no fear. If a football team takes the field and they're 14-point underdogs, they don't feel like losers. A good team feels like they just haven't won yet.

That's what being a good leader requires. Leaders deliver messages of confidence and calm. We aren't failing. Our imperfections won't destroy us. We still have tremendous advantages. We must recognize and exploit them. Victory is a mindset. We know how to make it ours.

Your people are watching you. They are assessing you, judging you, wondering what you are going to deliver and how. How do you value yourself? How do you conduct yourself? You show them through actions what you are made of. At Vaughan-Bassett, we do that by investing in the company and refusing to leave. We also prove our commitment in other ways. We share our vision by clearly explaining the challenges ahead. We talk to people and tell them where we're going and invite them to come along. When you let people know you have a plan and you don't intend to see it fail— that purges the whole organization of fear. That communication is powerful. It's team-building. It's fear-slaying. It works.

NOT TOO BIG TO MESS UP

There is a tendency to see competitors as supermen. They are not, no more than we are.

All companies have challenges. We see it every day. Volkswagen tried to trick the pollution control device. BP dumped a huge load of oil into the Gulf of Mexico in the Deepwater Horizon spill. BP's was an accident, while Volkswagen's was on purpose. But someone has to come in and make things right, no matter how the screwup happened. Customers, environmentalists, and government officials all have a right to ask: What the hell are they going to do? The CEO would rather not close the whole company. Caught in this position, a leader must do five things:

- Admit the mistake.
- Take responsibility.
- Correct the problem.

- Compensate the people who were hurt.
- Rebuild public confidence that it won't happen again.

All this takes enormous calm under pressure. How would you like to be the new CEO of Volkswagen and have to face up to all the questions swirling around that company? Whatever you do, you can't panic. You have to step forward and say: "We're going to correct this. We're going to work on it right now."

Compared to what Volkswagen and BP faced or still do, most of our companies have it easy. We're just banging against our competitors and trying to expand our market share. I still talk to many people in the industry who sound like they've given up. It seems almost unpatriotic to me. Americans have never been a give-up country. That's not who we are! I hope it never is! That doesn't mean we won't need to close some factories, but we won't throw our hands over our heads and just quit. Americans aren't quitters!

I've always liked what General Patton said: "Americans play to win at all times. I wouldn't give a hoot in hell for a man who lost and laughed."

"CAREFUL, KID! GET DOWN FROM THERE!"

I'll give you a good example of how we didn't panic after discovering a potential safety crisis. I'm convinced we've also saved some young lives. We may never know. This involves what people in the furniture industry call "tipability."

Every two weeks, on average, a child is crushed to death somewhere in America due to televisions falling off a piece of furniture or the furniture tipping over. These cases are horrible. Often, a child pulls out the drawers of a dresser or chest and then climbs up the front like a ladder. Suddenly, the piece tips forward, falling on top of the child.

Along with the two dozen or more annual fatalities—there were 40 tragic deaths in the peak year of 2011—another 2,000 children a year are injured severely enough to require hospital treatment. The victims are most often children three, four, or five years old—old enough to climb, not old enough to grasp the danger. More children under the age of nine have died this way than from the highly publicized ignition-switch problems in General Motors cars, the U.S. Consumer Product Safety Commission points out.

Accidents like these are nothing new, but the industry has seen a fresh rash of them in recent years due to the changes in flat-screen TVs and the introduction of full-extension drawers—drawers that slide all the way out, usually on ball bearings. They were developed for desks and kitchen cabinets, where the pieces aren't as tall and, in the case of kitchen cabinets, are usually bolted together and also bolted to the wall or floor. Full-extension drawers can be handy if you store your steak knives all the way in the back.

But just as a matter of physics, they can be dangerous in a tall, unsecured dresser or chest, especially if there are small children in the house. That's why at Vaughan-Bassett, our chest and dresser drawers are full access, not "full extension." They come out a maximum of 80 percent—plenty to access clothes and other bedroom items and far less risky to have in your home. To us, it's a nonnegotiable safety issue, though I'm sure we lose some sales when customers insist on full-extension drawers.

As the tip-over deaths mounted, some companies kept selling products with full-extension drawers. Eventually, it came to the attention of the Consumer Product Safety Commission. We didn't panic.

We have a policy in place that we're comfortable with. We've worked with the American Society of Testing and Materials, to devise what's known as the "fifty-pound test." Our furniture is tested, making sure no piece will tip over even with fifty pounds of weight in the drawer.

Not long ago, a representative from the Consumer Product Safety Commission called a meeting with the industry. Wyatt represented us.

"These accidents have got to stop," the woman from Washington said. "Unfortunately, there are no domestic manufacturers left in America we can work with." Of course Wyatt let her know they could absolutely work with Vaughan-Bassett. "We've been here since 1919," my son said. "We want to work with you."

That's what a calm, responsible company does when an issue arises.

THE LEADER'S ACTION PLAN: CHAPTER 8

INOCULATE AGAINST PANIC

MAKE YOUR OWN BAD DECISIONS—AND GOOD ONES, TOO. Panic comes mostly from allowing other people to sweep you along. The best antidote to panic is self-confidence. "I'm not saying I'm right all the time, but I trust my judgment to decide." Remember the old question your mother used to use? "If Johnny jumped off a bridge, would you jump, too?" Don't get pushed into the water by someone else's panic.

LIVING WITH UNCERTAINTY REQUIRES COURAGE AND CALM. You've been around people who are panicking. You know how hard it is not to be swept up. The good news is that calm is just as contagious as panic is, and the people around you will appreciate it a whole lot more. Practice calm in small ways. Don't flip out over little setbacks. Pretty soon you'll be calmly handling dire challenges and reaping the rewards.

KNOW YOUR RISK TOLERANCE. People are wired differently when it comes to courting danger. Some consider risk exhilarating. Others find it excruciating. Wherever you fall on that spectrum, you'll never eliminate risk entirely, not if you are facing large challenges or hoping to achieve

anything significant at all. But knowing your tolerance will
position you to make sound decisions you can live with—
and then calmly handle the results.

**UNMASK THE SCARED-EST COMMON
DENOMINATOR.** There's a panicker in every crowd.
Every organization has one: the person worrying the loudest,
the person who refuses to take any chances, the person who
is always worried what others might think. Don't let that
person define the issues or narrow your response.

Chapter 9

Teamwork and Communication

We didn't order our employees to do anything. We didn't threaten anyone. We didn't stand over them and force them to behave a certain way. There wasn't any secret algorithm. We communicated, they communicated, and everyone understood. We told them this is where we are. This is what the Chinese have done. This is what we need to achieve. Our people grasped the threat we were facing and understood what had to be done. Just as much as we did, they wanted to make sure the factory stayed busy and everyone remained employed. They knew where the inefficiencies were in their equipment and in their procedures. They made adjustments and corrections. They figured out how to do it, and they got it done.

We need each other, employees and management. There is no other way. With the kinds of challenges we constantly face, top-down, dictatorial pronouncements aren't going to win anyone's loyalty.

I can bark only so loudly. I know only so much. When it comes to making furniture, people who've spent decades on a production line have talents I can never match. They have insights to offer, shortcuts to share, inventive problem-solving techniques that are certainly worth considering. If our employees aren't on board with what we are doing, there is no chance we will ever succeed.

None at all.

From the very beginning, I knew that if we were going to reach our potential, our company must be less of a rigid hierarchy and more of a fully engaged team. And this will never happen unless we communicate openly, from the top to the bottom and inside out. Information has to flow in all directions. We need to exchange ideas like intelligent human beings. We're in this together. We must communicate, communicate, communicate. That openness and mutuality, I am convinced, is how we foster teamwork, and that teamwork will make us better than anyone.

Early in the anti-dumping saga, a Chinese company decided to copy our contemporary bedroom suite. I don't mean they were inspired by our sleek design and created something similar of their own. This was a straight-out knock-off job. We could tell just by looking that they'd cut a few corners on materials and production techniques.That would explain the lower prices. But to some value-conscious furniture buyers, these pieces looked pretty similar to ours—and they cost 20-percent less.

How would we react? We harnessed the power of communication and teamwork. We had a frank conversation with the world's greatest experts on Vaughan-Bassett furniture, our own employees.

We placed one of our suites in the employee cafeteria, and beside it we set up the Chinese version. We called the employees in.

"This is a significant threat to our business," I said of the lower-cost imports. "If we are going to compete, we must step up our production by twenty percent. That's the only way we can bring our prices down sufficiently."

A 20 percent speed-up is an enormous challenge in a factory that is already running efficiently. And we had to do it with the people and equipment that we already had. I laid this all on the line.

"We can't immediately increase your pay," I said, "and we can't bring in more people. The company is still going to lose money on this suite. But if we do this, I believe we can keep everyone working on a full schedule, and we can keep our factory running." Basically, what I was proposing to our employees was blood, toil, tears, and sweat.

"Before you agree to anything," I cautioned, "I want you all to think about this seriously. This is real commitment here." Then, I left the room.

I was called back later, and one of the employees, speaking for the group, said to me, "We've all discussed it, and we have decided overwhelmingly we want to do this."

"Don't tell me you can get twenty percent extra and then don't do it," I warned.

"No, no," they said. "We can do it. We just want one thing. We want a loudspeaker system that will tell us every hour if we are ahead or behind."

That was easy. "You got it," I said.

As I stood there in front of our team, I could already see the wheels spinning in people's heads, imagining possible adjustments to our usual production techniques and ways of getting things done more quickly. The guys carried that Chinese furniture back into the factory, where they took apart every piece, studying the techniques the foreign workers used. Then our people devised their own methods for shaving 20 percent off their production time.

And they did it, just like they said they would.

PEOPLE WANT TO JOIN PRODUCTIVE TEAMS

We didn't order our employees to do anything. We didn't threaten anyone. We didn't stand over them and force them to behave a certain way. There wasn't any secret algorithm. We communicated, they communicated, and everyone understood. We told them, This is where we are. This is what the Chinese have done. This is what we need to achieve. Our people grasped the threat we were facing and understood what had to be done. Just as much as we did, they wanted to make sure the factory stayed busy and everyone remained employed. They knew where the inefficiencies were in their equipment and in their procedures. They made adjustments and corrections. They figured out how to do it, and they got it done.

Inclusion builds loyalty.

The army taught me that if a soldier is going to risk his life, he wants to know what he might be dying for. You have to

- Tell him the mission.
- Explain why it's important.
- Identify the enemy.
- Describe how the mission will be executed.
- Let the soldier know he isn't alone.

His buddies are there. You are there. The nation back home is rooting for him. Something grand is at stake.

It's no different in business. We've got to communicate and foster a sense of joint purpose. Over the years we have created some structures for doing that. Once every month or two, we have an all-employee meeting. We don't wait for these meetings to report to the employees. We try to do that every day and every week. But these monthly gatherings help foster a sense that we are all trying to achieve the same goals. We go into the factory and stand on a platform in the middle of the cabinet room. Or sometimes we hold the meetings in the cafeteria and break everyone into two or three groups. However we do it, over the course of an hour and a half, we meet with every employee. We invite their questions and comments, and we share our own perspective on what's going on.

Some of this is basic human decency with a dollop of country Christianity tossed in. Treat people like you want to be treated. Respect the humanity of everyone. Some of it is just enlightened capitalism. The employees know things that can help the business. Make them feel part of it. Chances are, they will speak up. They'll give you good ideas. They will extend themselves. They'll make extra efforts to get involved.

When we were deciding whether to proceed with the dumping petition,

- We pulled the employees into the discussion.
- We explained to them what we were planning to do.
- We made sure they understood that we'd be taking on some powerful forces and that some people in the industry didn't agree with our approach.
- Then we took a vote of the employees.

There's actually a provision in the law that gives employees a chance to be heard before an anti-dumping petition is filed. We thought that was terrific, and we utilized it fully. Ninety-eight percent of our workers voted. All but a couple said, "Let's do it." Everyone who cast a ballot got a T-shirt imprinted with "I voted to save my job today."

Obviously, they were going to be supportive of our taking the leadership role within the industry to go after China. That approach contrasted sharply with what a lot of other companies were doing. Many were on the fence about the anti-dumping investigation or opposed it outright. Our boldness made our people feel like they were in the furniture industry vanguard. This feeling of being special carried over into their lives. Most of this industry is within a hundred-mile radius, the vast majority within two hundred miles. The hourly workers, as well as managers, all know people in other factories. Their neighbors knew they worked at Vaughan-Bassett. This made them stand out in their own communities.

HEALTHY COMMUNICATION

There are different ways to communicate that we are all on the same team. During the fiscal crisis, we noticed some employees were dropping out of the company's health insurance plan. Even those who kept their insurance weren't getting their usual checkups. When we inquired, people kept mentioning the $25 copay. They were waiting to get sicker before they went to see the doctor. They didn't want to pay the $25.

Over and above our regular insurance, we decided to provide a medical clinic where employees, spouses, and children could be treated at no charge. We contracted with the largest internal medical practice in Galax. They staff the clinic with physician assistants, overseen by doctors, and Vaughan-Bassett covers the costs.

This is a great benefit to the workforce. Where else can an employee see a doctor or a PA for free the first day on the job—and not just the employee but the employee's spouse and children too? Providing the clinic helps make us the corporate citizens we should be. It also helps keep our workers healthy, which benefits them and us. Doctors routinely find potential diabetes, early cardiac disease, pre-stroke conditions—all types of things. They counsel employees about the dangers of smoking and being overweight. Everyone gets a free physical exam annually.

In the beginning, there were some employees, mostly men, who didn't want to take the physical even though it was free. They could even get it on company time without being docked! Wyatt, along with Doug Brannock, who runs our insurance program, took on the job of encouraging these stubborn employees to get their physical exams. Wyatt and Doug got a lot of nodding and "I'll get around to it"—but there remained that last group of guys who wouldn't actually schedule their exams.

Sometimes, motivating people takes a more creative approach. "Turn this over to me," I said. I dictated a letter to the men who had refused the free physicals that qualified them and their families for free, primary health care at our clinic. I mentioned a looming dead-line. "If you don't get this physical within 60 days," I wrote, "you and your family no longer will be eligible to use our free clinic." Sheila mailed the letters on Friday—not to the men but to their wives. I let Mama take care of this!

On Monday morning, a row of guys were lined up like toy sol-diers outside the nurse's office, ready to sign up for that physical. Their weekends had obviously been most unpleasant. Show me any working-class mother who will pass up free primary health care for her family because of some stubborn husband who won't get a free physical he probably needs anyway. I doubt you can find a single one!

CRUISING TOGETHER AND APART

Teamwork isn't something that can be created and left alone. It is a living, breathing thing. The way a fire needs fuel and oxy-gen, teamwork has to be tended and stoked. You have to keep giving your people reasons to remain motivated and engaged. "Thunder and Lightning" was a great excitement-builder for our production people, especially when Shirley won that Harley and paid her mort-gage off. But we couldn't live off that forever. We needed a flow of fresh ideas.

Vaughan-Bassett wasn't the first company to use a cruise con-test to motivate the sales staff, but I like to think we brought our own special spin to the idea. Always put your own spin on things.

Bob Merriman, our sales manager, drew up targets for the sales staff for a six-month contest. If you hit your sales target, you and your spouse would be invited on a five-night Caribbean cruise, all expenses paid by the company. But that wasn't the whole story: If you hit a higher target, you were eligible for first class. And if you were the most outstanding salesperson of all, you'd be in the penthouse suite.

People seemed excited about the free cruise—so excited, in fact, that just two months in, every one of the salespeople had sold enough to qualify. Most of them, I noticed, would be traveling in "steerage," as I started calling the basic-level accommodations. To spur everyone on, I sent around an audiotape—these were still cassette days—to the salespeople's homes. Over the sound of seagulls, soft music, and gently crashing waves, a gentle voice announced breakfast in bed—followed immediately by a horrible, loud, clanging noise. Then a far rougher voice explained: "Unfortunately, your cabin is right next to the engine room. First-class cabins are located in the quieter and far more luxurious forward section of the ship."

That tape had exactly the intended effect. Within another month, nearly everyone on the sales staff had sold enough to qualify for a first-class cruise. But this created an issue for us. We still had three months to go.

"We have to give them something else to shoot for," Bob said to me. For another $60,000, he added, the cruise line would provide yet another level of onboard luxury perks.

"Let me think about it," I told Bob.

I did, and I came up with an alternate approach, one that wouldn't cost me $60,000.

"We'll have a group goal for the rest of the contest, not an individual goal, something the entire sales team can try to meet," I told Bob. "And the prize? If they meet the new target, I won't go on the cruise."

I had Sheila type up a letter to the salespeople. I told them how much I was looking forward to joining them on this wonderful adventure. I explained that I'd be right there with them for every meal, every cocktail, every hour in the ship's casino. Of course, we'd have to put some time aside for company business, reviewing next year's budget, assessing our sales technique, sitting through some presentations on long-term industry trends.

"Now if for some reason you would prefer I not join you, just meet Bob's new staff-wide sales goal.

"In that case, I will wish you *bon voyage* and remain at home."

It was a highly ambitious target. But two days before the ship sailed, the sales staff met it. I sent a follow-up note, saying how sorry I was that I wouldn't be joining them. "Please, try to have fun without me," I wrote.

From all I could tell, they had a blast without me! They returned to work excited and motivated and proposing new ideas. "So sorry you couldn't make it," they wrote in a follow-up note to me, and I'm absolutely certain they were fibbing.

That's how to spur motivation.

You have to keep coming up with new ways of getting it done, and they'd better be exciting. If the idea doesn't excite you, chances are it won't excite them. Don't make your people think, *This isn't worth the effort.* The cruise worked because people were motivated to be part of that adventure—and even more motivated to make sure I didn't come. And that last part didn't cost us a dime.

RESPONSIBILITY, A TWO-WAY STREET

Being part of a team also carries responsibilities—for everyone. And that means when there is pain, we try to spread it around.

Before we launched our Barnburners and the factory was still on short time, Doug, Wyatt, and I gave up our bonuses. The workers were being asked to suffer, we figured, and so should we.

We place expectations on our employees, too. We treat them like adults, include them in major decisions, treat them professionally, and handle disagreements maturely. So they should be to work on time, right?

Factories are especially dependent on 100 percent attendance—or close to it. Like basketball, mass production is by its nature a team sport. You wouldn't send four players onto a basketball court and expect to win a championship. It's the same in a factory. There could be seventy or eighty people on a conveyor line. To make furniture, we need them to be there. Even a handful of missing employees can really mess up our production.

This was an ongoing problem for us, but I finally got an idea about how to deal with it from the hardworking wife of one of our more troubled employees.

One morning, while I was at Bassett's Mount Airy plant, I had to dismiss one of our maintenance workers. We had given him several chances, but the man was an alcoholic, and he kept messing up. We couldn't risk an impaired worker causing an accident, so I discharged him.

That day at lunchtime, his wife showed up at my desk, asking me to reconsider. She and I were having a perfectly cordial conversation when all at once she looked at her watch, stood up, and rushed out.

Was it something I said? I wondered to myself. But late that afternoon, she was back. Now I was really confused. "Ma'am, you left," I said.

"I had to," she told me. "I didn't want to lose my bonus."

"What do you mean?" I asked her.

She worked at another manufacturing plant in Mount Airy, she said. "If we have perfect attendance during the week—it must be perfect and no excuses are accepted—I get a bonus check. I can't miss that!"

I'd never heard of a company doing that before, and I felt a tinge of envy. I wished all our employees shared this woman's concern about missing even a few minutes of work. I wanted to find out more.

The next morning, I called the company's president and asked him to explain to me exactly how their absentee program worked. He was happy to.

"We give our employees a bonus for perfect attendance," he said, just as the woman had told me. "All our people are eligible." He gave me the details.

"Perfect means perfect, John," he explained. "You can never have a reason for not being there. If it's a grandmother's funeral, you'll find out one day the person has six grandmothers. What you say is, 'I'm sorry you had to go to your grandmother's funeral. You start working toward the bonus again next week.' Our perfect-attendance calendar goes from Monday morning until Friday afternoon. It's been very effective in keeping down our absentee rates."

We put our own program in place at Vaughan-Bassett, beginning with a wage increase of 5 percent: 2 percent on the employee's regular wages and 3 percent as an attendance bonus. They are able to get that extra 3 percent one, two, three, or four weeks out of a month. We pay the bonus checks monthly, by separate check, based on how many weeks of perfect attendance the employee has. They get their regular pay and then they get a separate check that they can look at and say, "That's what I made by having perfect attendance." It has proven to be a very effective method of combatting absences and tardiness. The attendance bonus at Vaughan-Bassett is currently up to 14 percent.

Our absenteeism went from 5 percent or more down to less than 2 percent. Now, at 7 a.m. when the whistle blows, virtually everybody's on the line ready to go, which makes us a lot more efficient.

I was on the floor not long ago when our foremen were handing out the checks.

"You get your bonus check?" I asked a woman named Myrtle.

"All four weeks," she said.

"I'll bet your husband really likes those bonus checks," I said.

She just about died laughing. She held up her regular payroll check.

"He knows about this one," she said. "But he doesn't even know I get this one," she added, holding up the perfect-attendance bonus. "This is my pantyhose money."

We have to learn how to incentivize American workers. Praise is important, but something tangible is often better. People love that extra bonus check. Something special. Something off to the side. Do we still have some issues with tardiness and absenteeism? The answer is yes, but it's a fraction of what we used to have. Once we tell people what we expect and make them feel responsible, they tend to take care of themselves.

Some people say the American Dream isn't relevant anymore, but I don't believe that. I think most people do believe in the possibility of a brighter future for themselves and their families, and most are willing to work for it. When somebody stands in front of them and says they are committed to making that happen, people will listen. You just have to tell them where you're going and how you're going to get there.

THE LEADER'S ACTION PLAN: CHAPTER 9

MAKING THE TEAM

TO GET LOYALTY, YOU HAVE TO GIVE LOYALTY.
We constantly ask our employees to do more. Work harder.
Work smarter. Work faster. Do more with less. In return,
we have to treat them as the core of the business, which
they are. We have to pay them, appreciate them, and protect
them as well as we humanly can. Loyalty really is a two-way
street.

TALK AND ACT. Actions may speak louder than words,
but you need both to build an effective team. We tell our
employees they are important to us. We keep saying it. We
show it by seeking their input, investing in the company, and
sharing the rewards with them. This isn't tokenism. It's how
we do business. And we keep telling our unique story, inside
the organization and out.

DEFINE THE TEAM BROADLY. We're all in this
together—all of us! Management, employees, customers,
vendors, neighbors, friends, industry colleagues—and the
families of all of them. When something happens inside
a company, it affects far more than the owners and the
employees. Share your story with everyone. They are all
potential allies. Keep as many people as possible involved.

TREAT YOUR PEOPLE LIKE PEOPLE WITH LIVES.
They have them, you know? Kids to look after, spouses to
support, health to be concerned about, mortgages to pay. All
of that affects the energy and attention they will have for
their jobs. As an employer, you can't resolve all life's issues.
But you can recognize everyone has some, and the job
doesn't always have to exacerbate them.

Chapter 10

Reinvest Constantly

This is our physical heritage. We have a responsibility to maintain it—for ourselves and for the generations to come. Without it, how can we possibly expect to compete in this era of globalization? China, India, the nations of Southeast Asia and the Middle East—they're all investing like gangbusters in their infrastructure, while we keep falling further and further behind. Without reliable roads and bridges, we can't move our goods to market. Without decent mass transit, our major cities will be choked with traffic gridlock. Without secure dams and levees, we're always one natural disaster away from utter catastrophe.

I have what just may be the most beautiful daily commute in America.

I might get an argument from people who drive California's Pacific Coast Highway, Colorado's San Juan Skyway, or the Overseas Highway in the Florida Keys. We do have some amazingly scenic rides in this great country of ours. But twice a day, between my home in Roaring Gap, North Carolina, and our factory in Galax, Virginia, I take the Blue Ridge Parkway.

I know how blessed I am.

Winding 469 miles from the Great Smoky Mountains in North Carolina to Shenandoah National Park in Virginia, this toll-free, two-lane roadway is actually America's longest linear park. The route includes stunning mountain overlooks, colonial-era cabins and hunting grounds, flowering shrubs and wildflowers, and all kinds of animals darting everywhere. My little stretch takes me past the Cumberland Knob recreation area, across the North Carolina–Virginia line, and over enough American history to fill an Advanced Placement high school textbook. That state line was surveyed by a 1749 party that included Peter Jefferson, Thomas Jefferson's father. The road and the land on both sides of it are maintained by the National Park Service.

Let me rephrase that last point: They are *supposed to be* maintained by the National Park Service.

Staff reductions, budget cuts, competing priorities, and advancing age (the parkway was established in 1935 as part of

169

Franklin Delano Roosevelt's New Deal) have conspired to leave this ambitious public works project a cracked, bumpy, potholed mess. Much as I enjoy the drive, I must grip the steering wheel to dodge weather-beaten road hazards along the way. God and our industrious ancestors left us this national treasure. Here in the second decade of the twenty-first century, we haven't been able to keep it in passably decent shape.

Just to be clear, this is not some out-of-way, seldom-used vestige of America's past. Though not officially a national park, the parkway was the most visited unit of the National Park Service in all but two of the last sixty years. Makes you wonder how they are maintaining the facilities that are less popular. If I were looking for a new business to start, I really might consider a tire repair service somewhere near the parkway. I'm sure the phone would ring around the clock.

So how did this happen? Why is the Blue Ridge Parkway in such ragged shape? It isn't that the federal road crews don't know how to fill potholes. It isn't that American drivers are any rougher on the roads than other drivers. It's that we as a nation no longer consider maintaining our infrastructure to be an important priority. Clearly, sufficient resources aren't being devoted to get the job done.

Honestly, how hard could it be?

OUR CRUMBLING AMERICA

I bring up the Blue Ridge Parkway not just to air a personal gripe, though I do feel better already. But this one battered roadway is emblematic of a far larger problem that plagues organizations in America, be they businesses, schools, utilities, or governments.

From coast to coast, we do a terrible job maintaining the vital infrastructure that supports our economy and makes our country work. Roads. Bridges. Levees. Water projects. Power grids. Sewer systems. Data and telecommunications networks. Airports. Seaports. Rail lines. Educational institutions. Police departments. All the gritty, unglamorous systems that support what our people and businesses need and use daily. This is our physical heritage. We have a responsibility to maintain it—for ourselves and for the generations to come. Without it, how can we possibly expect to compete in this era of globalization? China, India, the nations of Southeast Asia and the Middle East—they're all investing like gangbusters in their infrastructure, while we keep falling further and further behind. Without reliable roads and bridges, we can't move our goods to market. Without decent mass transit, our major cities will be choked with traffic gridlock. Without secure dams and levees, we're always one natural disaster away from utter catastrophe.

And then there's our twenty-fourth-in-the-world broadband. That's where the latest annual report issued by the UN Broadband Commission ranked the United States. As advanced as we like to think we are, only 84 percent of our population has access to the Internet now. In Iceland, it's almost 97 percent. Also outranking us are other countries including Qatar, Bahrain, and the United Arab Emirates. Even Canada does better. And here's what really worries me: The United States isn't improving its status. In one year, our country slipped further behind by four spots. It's hard to do business and claim we are the most competitive and technologically advanced nation in the world when our broadband access, speed, and cost rank below South Korea's. Without a state-of-the-art communications system, our most promising and profitable industries—

finance, tech, health care, not to mention what's left of our manufacturing core—will be forced to operate at a constant disadvantage against foreign competitors.

This is already happening, and it's not getting better. It's getting worse.

This is just dumb. It's irresponsible to future generations. It's hurting us already. It strangles our economy. It limits our growth. Whatever money we're saving by skipping infrastructure support, we'll end up paying many times over in missed opportunity and lost productivity. We may not be spending, but others are. We're handing them the club to beat us with. Does anyone really think we don't need to move goods smoothly, to get our people around, to communicate reliably, and to live safely in the world? If we let those facilities deteriorate, we will constantly be struggling at a huge disadvantage, lacking the basic tools to succeed. It really is time to reinvest in America.

INFRASTRUCTURE INVESTING
STARTS AT HOME

How do I know all this? I learned it in a direct and personal way: from making the commitment to modernize our company, and watching what happened as a result. Investing in our infrastructure was one of the decisions that saved Vaughan-Bassett.

All through the 1990s, we'd been talking about modernizing the plant in Galax—funding capital improvements that would make us more efficient and more competitive. This was going to be expensive. We knew that. We'd have to borrow money. We didn't like taking on debt. We finally did it, starting in 1997—and what an impact it made!

You want figures? I'll give you the figures.

In 1996, the company had sales of $73.3 million. That year, we spent a paltry $1.6 million on capital improvements and had operating profits of $5.5 million.

We made the leap in 1997. After much discussion, the managers and the board members could see that globalization was coming. We recognized that the competition was only getting tougher. The big Asian tsunami hadn't hit yet, but it was certainly gathering and we could feel the breeze. In 1997, our capital spending more than tripled from the previous year, to $5.2 million. Our sales rose to $83.6 million. Our profits spiked to $11.1 million.

In 1998, we pushed even harder and invested even more. Our capital spending went to $7.7 million, and all that new equipment was having a practical, provable impact. Our sales climbed to $107 million, our profits to $15.2 million.

In 1999, we did even more: We spent $14.4 million on infrastructure projects, and look what happened: Our sales leaped to $156.9 million, our profits to $20.9 million.

Then, the tsunami hit.

In 2000, our capital investment was $6.1 million, down from the peak but still significant. That year's sales were still very strong: $163.4 million, though profits were squeezed a bit. They came in at $9.9 million.

That investment wasn't enough to shield us entirely from the pressures that shook our whole industry. But it was as clear to me then as it is to me now: If we had not invested this money and become as efficient as we did, the cheap Chinese competition that hit our shore would have wiped us out like it wiped out so many others. We had to face some very tough competitors. Most of our American colleagues, who hadn't made the necessary investments, decided these

competitors were just too tough. Many of those American companies disappeared. But we had invested, and we were ready for what
came next. We had a state-of-the-art facility and people who knew
how to run it. That gave us a fighting chance.

To me, the analogy is clear: We must reinvest in America the
same way and for the same reasons we invested in our firm: To stay
ahead of the competition and because if we don't, we will inevitably
fall behind. Honestly, our country has no other reasonable choice.

HOW BAD IS IT, REALLY?

You think I'm exaggerating the threat our nation faces? Perhaps
the national numbers will convince you otherwise.

Public infrastructure investment is now at a twenty-year low—
2.4 percent of America's gross national product, half what it was
fifty years ago. The American Society of Civil Engineers charts
this sort of thing. After an exhaustive study, the association gave
our nation's infrastructure a barely passing, D+ grade. Potential
investors have started comparing America's rickety infrastructure
to that of a Third World country—and not in a flattering way. Is this
really how our country is going to stay on top? In a recent report,
the Council on Foreign Relations warned somberly: "The United
States has huge unpaid bills coming due for its infrastructure. A
generation of investments in world-class infrastructure in the mid-
twentieth century is now reaching the end of its useful life."

Added the council's analysts: "Despite the pressing infrastructure investment needs of the United States, federal infrastructure
policy is paralyzed by partisan wrangling over massive infrastructure bills that fail to move through Congress."

No wonder it feels like we are falling behind!

Fixing this won't be cheap. Since spending has been put off for so long, some experts say that just to get even, we should expect to spend at least $2.3 trillion—that's a 2, a 3, and nine zeros or 2,300 billion—over the next decade. Other estimates run as high as $3.6 trillion by 2020. It's a lot of money, whatever the precise figure is. And we haven't been getting much help from Washington. When it comes to delaying, ignoring, and reducing infrastructure investment, our political leaders have turned out to be excellent enablers. Too bad they haven't been as proficient at getting things done. They certainly haven't solved much!

Everyone in Washington seems to agree that our lack of infrastructure investment is a dire issue that must be confronted immediately. We need a "twenty-first-century infrastructure," to use President Obama's favorite term. Leaders in Congress, Republicans and Democrats, echo the dire warnings and beg for action. But month after month, year after year, they make very little progress down that (badly potholed) road. They can't agree on what should be included, which priorities should come first, and how it should be paid for. Instead of cobbling together a sensible plan, they get tangled in all the usual Washington squabbles: highways versus public-transit, schools versus prisons, oil and coal versus renewable energy, the natural environment versus economic development. These are all interesting debates. But a trillion-dollar, bipartisan infrastructure plan keeps going nowhere in Congress, never getting through the House and Senate, never landing on the president's desk. And America's crumbling infrastructure crumbles some more. No one can say when Washington will finally do something, but everyone knows where doing nothing will lead—to worse roads, collapsing bridges, weaker levees, more blackouts, dumpier airports, and on and on and on.

Here's what I've learned from more than a half century in the business world: You can dream up a killer concept. You can build the most useful product imaginable. You can create frantic consumer demand. But if you can't get your product to the customer because the road is impassable or the power went off or the levee broke, you don't have anything of value at all. That's the infrastructure crisis America faces today.

We have to face the consequences of our neglect. We must quit feeling sorry for ourselves and instead say, "We need to compete. That means investing in ourselves. Let's get out there and do it." I say, "Borrow the money if we have to."

I am proud to say that investing in our own infrastructure has been a guiding principle at Vaughan-Bassett, one I feel especially good about. We invest in the latest equipment. We invest in our physical plant. We invest in new technology. Most important of all, we invest in our people—their training, their safety, their health, their morale, their productivity. We don't view this as a waste of money or a threat to the bottom line. We view it for what it is, an investment in a future we all hope to share. And, yes, we've been willing to borrow when we needed to, but we've invested more than $90 million to keep our factory one of the most modern in the country. Thankfully, we had no sequestration to worry about, so we had an easier time with the bankers than Congress does.

You'll see something similar in most growing businesses everywhere—a willingness to invest in the future. You won't see it in declining organizations. Continued success has to be fertilized constantly—with ideas, energy, creativity, and of course money.

BEG, BORROW, OR STEAL—JUST DO IT

As important as this is, we should borrow the money to pay for it if that's what it takes to get the job done. I understand all the arguments against this. I have heard them from my friends:

- The federal government spends too much already, although the budget deficit has been coming down.
- Borrowing's a bad idea—you have to pay back all those loans.
- Because of sequestration, Congress has far less spending flexibility than it used to.
- Raising the debt ceiling is always a huge political ordeal.

Here's the problem with all those arguments: In this case, they aren't persuasive. In this case, the benefits of borrowing outweigh the risks. Most homeowners take out mortgages. We have to invest in our future the same way.

A lot of our current spending goes to fund social programs, the safety net our government provides for its people. I'm not saying we have the perfect one or we should add or subtract from it. That debate will follow its own path. As a practical matter, social spending will be what it is. But social programs do not pay for themselves, and infrastructure investment does. It creates jobs. It strengthens the economy. It helps create a legacy for future generations. It makes us more competitive today. Think of infrastructure spending as the GI Bill of Interior Maintenance. It's taxpayer money intelligently deployed. It's exactly what the government should do.

After World War II, America had an army of returning veterans—literally an army—men and women who had defeated the Germans and the Japanese. They had done their jobs and were ready to be absorbed into civilian society and get on with the rest of their lives. The GI Bill—controversial at first but in retrospect hugely popular—helped these vets get an education, buy homes, start businesses, and become successful, productive members of a growing society. That's what it did for them. What it did for the country is even more extraordinary. It boosted the economy. It built the modern middle class. It turned the twentieth century into the American Century. It solidified our nation's place in the postwar world. Those returning veterans, with the investment the nation made in them, truly helped America win the peace. The lasting result was decades and decades of prosperity, the likes of which the world has never seen.

The GI Bill was one of the smartest things we've ever done as a nation. It paid for itself many times over. Rebuilding America's physical infrastructure is a challenge of a different sort, but the payback will be spectacular. Why shouldn't we borrow money to achieve something like that? It would pay for itself! It will leave us with better airports, better roads, better Internet service, better you-name-it—part of the cost of entry in this increasingly global age. Think of it as America investing in itself. What better investment could the nation make? Once we start collecting the taxes on all these projects, they will pay for themselves many times over. And now is the perfect time. Look how low interest rates are. We should be out in the market borrowing hundreds of billions of dollars. Infrastructure should be the focus of a twenty-first-century GI Bill.

I've put a lot of thought into this. Everybody looks to the federal government, but the federal government doesn't have to cover the cost alone. Some of it can be apportioned to the states. I've got news for you. The states have borrowing power, too, and many of them know how to use it. Washington can go to the states and say, "We will spend more in your state if you will match it." If some states say, "We don't want to participate," we'll say, "Fine. You don't have to. We'll send the money to Oklahoma or Arkansas"—or some other state that's willing to match it and wants the extra benefits. "We'll let them kick your butt." Believe me, states that see the value in participating won't be hard to find.

ROADS, BRIDGES—AND ESPECIALLY PEOPLE

America does not live by roads, bridges, and power grids alone. Our vital infrastructure is human, too. Even if we get the most gleaming physical structures on earth—who knows, we may get them one day!—they won't be much good to us if our people aren't trained and available. So, yes, we need to invest in our human infrastructure as well.

This means community colleges. And job training programs. And internships. And apprentice programs where experienced workers can take the time to show the newbies how to do these jobs well. As American manufacturing has gone more high-tech, it takes well-educated, computer-savvy employees to assemble, operate, and repair this cutting-edge machinery. We're long past the days where some half-alert guy could stand next to a piece of equipment and keep up with everything going on. Frankly, I'm not sure that day ever really existed. But if it did, it's long gone now.

At our plant—and other up-to-date plants across the country— the employees are performing a series of complex tasks. They are constantly making decisions, tweaking the orders, adjusting, prodding, recalculating, applying metrics, making judgment calls, and interacting intelligently with the latest technology. There are few mindless tasks in our plant—and no mindless people. Everything we do requires a measure of intelligence, skill, and training.

So where do we go to get these people? And how are we going to keep them? It's not as easy as it sounds. Because of all the lay-offs in our industry, there was a pool of available labor. There were people who wanted to work. Nothing pleases me more than finding a place for someone who was employed in the industry, loved it, did well, and got squeezed out because of a round of layoffs or a factory closing or another company's throwing in the towel for good. The workers didn't cause these large trends in the economy. They just suffered the results. Some terrific people have come to us from other companies that don't build furniture anymore. We are lucky and grateful to have them.

But the pool of skilled furniture workers is not as deep as you might think, and it certainly won't last forever. As people have lost their jobs, many of them migrated into other industries or moved to other states in search of work. When they go, they take with them their extraordinary knowledge, their years of experience, and their deep personal relationships, which often can never be recaptured. As the industry has shrunk, one of the biggest tragedies is all the talent that's slipped away. You can't expect people to stick around forever. Whether they want to or not, they have to get on with their lives. Think about the implications of this for the long-term future of our industry and of manufacturing overall. There comes a point where if someone tried to open a huge plant in Virginia or North Carolina, or any other state, they'd have a tough time finding the people to staff it. That deep pool of talents will have long washed away. That hasn't happened yet, not entirely, but you can see the trend. It is a looming reality in our field. The same is true in other threatened industries. We need employers to protect this important human resource. Talent has to be nourished and supported. That takes jobs.

And once you have well-trained workers, the education continues. The technology keeps advancing. The competition learns new tricks. Staying even isn't an option. Our knowledge has to be constantly expanding ahead of our competition. So do our techniques. This means constantly investing in on-the-job training. Otherwise, we are certain to fall behind. Our business is successful only if we stay at the top of our game.

That's why we devote so much effort and expense to training. It's why I am so supportive of government effort—local, state, and federal—to help create the workforce of tomorrow. That's why cutting training and education funds, even when times are tough, is such a shortsighted policy in the global economy of a country that very much wants to compete. Like investing in physical infrastructure, investing in people pays itself back many times over.

In all this, of course, government can be helpful by building and sustaining the infrastructure. But individual companies and individual industries must always do their part. The role of the private sector is a crucial one. We have to invest for the same reasons our government does. Our future depends on it!

PUBLIC AND PRIVATE, WORKING AS A TEAM

The need to build and maintain our national infrastructure is so obvious and so great that even Harvard Business School is paying attention. Some of the top people there decided to address the issue in a major way. They summoned seventy-three CEOs, mayors, governors, labor leaders, university presidents, and policy experts—and a handful of Harvard professors—to address what many of them agreed was the single largest challenge facing the U.S. economy. This was an impressive group, well stocked with people who have hands-on experience wrestling with major business and economic issues beyond just studying them: Sam's Club president Rosalind Brewer, Honeywell chairman and CEO David Cote, AFL-CIO policy director Damon Silvers, American Red Cross president Gail McGovern, former homeland security secretary Janet Napolitano, former Indiana governor Mitch Daniels, former Massachusetts governor Deval Patrick, former Michigan governor John Engler, Minneapolis mayor Betsy Hodges, and Salt Lake City mayor Ben McAdams.

The challenges are many, the experts conceded. Congressional gridlock. The pressure from globalization that handicaps America's skilled workforce. But companies and governments, they agreed, still have immense power in their hands. "Leaders of all stripes understand that our best bet is for all sectors—including business, government, education, nonprofit, and labor—to work together to rebuild the commons," said Jan Rivkin, who cochairs Harvard's U.S. Competitiveness Project. The potential prize? Millions of new middle-class jobs.

Sitting together in Cambridge, Massachusetts, this diverse group discovered much the same thing we'd learned on the factory floor in Galax, Virginia. Our economy is being squeezed by three factors:

- **Globalization and technological progress:** American workers are competing with increasingly skilled workers around the globe and against improving automation in the workplace.

- **Institutional gridlock:** Changes in America's political and economic institutions, such as polarization in Congress, have left our nation far less capable of responding to change.
- **Underinvestment in infrastructure:** Exactly!

The assembled leaders figured their call might not be heard unless they highlighted some promising examples of business and government working together, even in small ways, to rebuild what they called "America's commons." The commons—that's the Harvard word for infrastructure—is "the shared resources that countries and citizens rely on in order to be productive." By any name, it turns out these examples aren't so hard to find.

- In Salt Lake City, the local government is expanding preschool education through pay-for-success contracts with education providers.
- In Boston, the Massachusetts Life Sciences Center is providing tax incentives and other support for biotech and pharma companies.
- In Columbus, Ohio, the CEO-led Columbus Partnership has channeled the resources and expertise of the local business community to promote economic development and, increasingly, help city agencies tackle thorny issues like education reform.
- In North Carolina, Siemens Corporation is collaborating with Central Piedmont Community College to give students the training necessary to thrive at the company after graduation.

Rivkin rightly pointed out: "This work has already begun in cities and regions across the country, and the business community can play a critical role in leading and sustaining these initiatives over the long term."

Their specific suggestions weren't so different from ours:

- Improving training and education
- Building a more skilled workforce
- Establishing government policies that encourage entrepreneurship, such as sensible tax rates, rational regulation, and infrastructure investment
- Making a national commitment to rebuild our crumbling infrastructure

We might just have a place for some of those folks at Vaughan-Bassett.

THE LEADER'S ACTION PLAN: CHAPTER 10

INVEST UNTIL IT HURTS

KEEP INVESTING. When it comes to reinvestment—in old infrastructure or new technology—you are never really finished. To remain competitive in today's markets, you have to keep spending money, updating your equipment, training your people, marketing your brand. Even a brief interruption can be damaging. A longtime pullback in infrastructure investment really is the same as giving up.

THINGS WEAR OUT MORE QUICKLY NOW. Blame the race of technology. You replace your cell phone every year or two. That big-butt TV looks like it came from the Stone Age. So why should business technology stay fresh longer? Most of it doesn't. It constantly needs to be updated. This is expensive but unavoidable. There have been so many wonderful advances in technology, you can't ignore them. You have to use them effectively.

NO RESTING ON YOUR LAURELS. Feel good about what your business has achieved in previous years, decades, or centuries, if you've managed to survive that long. Whatever you were doing, it must have been working, right? But much of that legacy is of little use to you now. You have to compete and win in the marketplace every day. A legacy is wonderful. Treasure it. Now move on.

INVEST IN YOUR PEOPLE, NOT JUST YOUR MACHINES. Your employees really are the most valuable infrastructure you have. Why have shiny new equipment operated by broken-down employees? That's like building your dream house without laying a proper foundation. Make sure your people are trained. Teach them the latest technique. Give them the opportunities to grow their knowledge and careers.

Chapter 11

Make the Best of the Worst

Nothing is more painful in business than the need to lay off employees. Still, no company, certainly not ours, can ever say unequivocally, "We will never have layoffs, no matter what." But you can say this: "If we need to have layoffs, we'll do everything we can to avoid it, and if that doesn't work, we'll do it as humanely as possible. We'll try to find other places in the company for people who are displaced. We'll seek voluntary departures, offer severance payments, and give people as much notice as we possibly can." We owe our workers at least that much.

Even good companies sometimes do bad things.

Like many large retailers, Toys "R" Us was eager to cut costs. That wasn't unusual. Lots of companies feel that pressure today. What was truly shocking was the painful disregard the nation's largest toy seller, with 863 Toys "R" Us and Babies "R" Us stores across the United States, showed to its own employees.

Toys "R" Us was already known as a tough bargainer. Buying in huge volume. Marketing aggressively. But this latest maneuver was on another level entirely, provoking gasps even inside the company's suburban headquarters complex in Wayne, New Jersey.

Here's what happened: One morning in March 2015, a Toys "R" Us vice president summoned sixty-seven employees from the accounting department to a large conference room. He explained to the full-time employees that their jobs would be eliminated by the end of June. They were being replaced by workers in India, recruited by a labor broker in Bangalore called TCS. And one other thing: The replacement workers would soon be arriving in New Jersey, checking into a nearby La Quinta Inn, and spending a couple of weeks in the accounting department so the veteran U.S. workers could teach the newcomers how to do their jobs.

"We were asked to cooperate and show them respect and train them to do our individual job functions," a thirty-six-year-old accountant who'd been with the company a dozen years told the *New York Times*. "If you didn't cooperate, you would be asked to leave"—without any severance pay.

When the Indian workers showed up in the office, none of them seemed to have any special expertise or extraordinary skills. Their English was spotty. Their data training was basic. They certainly seemed to know less than the Americans they would soon replace, many of whom had been with Toys "R" Us for years or decades. The new Indian workers sat next to the American employees, shadowing every move the longtime employees made.

"He was watching me like a hawk," the twelve-year employee said of her replacement. "It took him a while to learn what I did…I felt like, 'Why am I sitting here showing this man how to do my job when they are taking it away from me and sending it to India?'"

To me, this was at least as bad as—maybe even worse than—what happened to many American furniture industry workers when they were dumped for Asian factory hands. At least our people didn't have to teach their replacements how to operate a rotary saw or a lacquer gun. Thank God for small favors, right? But the economic pressures on the two industries were quite similar. Toy making, like furniture making, had already largely gone overseas. Now the cost-cutters were coming for the headquarters staff. Once the job-napping gets rolling, the race to the bottom never ends.

It turned out that this technique was no aberration unique to Toys "R" Us. In fact, it represents a rapidly burgeoning trend. What makes it possible—and could be a scary portent of future maneuvers to come—is the expansive use of a U.S. visa program called H-1B. When Congress created the program in the last decade, the idea was to bring in college-educated foreigners with "highly specialized knowledge" that American workers didn't possess. The promise was that these workers would "not adversely affect the working conditions" or undercut the wages of American workers—

and would help American companies compete around the world. That in turn would create more American jobs.

Or so the theory went.

A FRAUD ON AMERICA

The reality was that of the 85,000 H-1B visas every year, a large share has gone to global outsourcing firms, who contract with companies as diverse as Walt Disney, Southern California Edison, and New York Life. As a result of claims filed by replaced workers, some companies have faced scrutiny from the U.S. Department of Labor over their use of H-1B visas and overseas outsourcing consultants. Federal labor investigators also opened probes against TCS and another India-based labor broker, Infosys, after Southern California Edison laid off more than five hundred technology workers.

The program "is plagued with fraud and abuse and is now a vehicle for outsourcing that deprives qualified American workers of their jobs," said Senator Richard Durbin, an Illinois Democrat, who was joined in his complaints by Alabama Republican Jeff Sessions. Chairman Chuck Grassley even called a hearing of the Senate Judiciary Committee to focus on the visas' abuse.

"The program was intended to serve employers who could not find the skilled workers they needed in the United States," said Grassley, a Republican from Iowa. "Over the years the program has become a government-assisted way for employers to bring in cheaper foreign labor, and now it appears these foreign workers take over—rather than complement—the U.S. workforce."

Now, if only Congress would act.

For American workers, these guest worker visas really are becoming a long trail of tears:

- At Cengage Learning, an educational publisher, thirty accountants in Ohio and Kentucky were laid off after spending four months training Indian workers from Cognizant, another major player in the outsourcing field. When the training sessions were done, the temporary workers headed back to India along with the Americans' old jobs. Cengage spokeswoman Susan Aspey said the company needed to install higher-grade accounting systems "quickly and efficiently," and the outsourcing consultant was able to help with that. The laid-off Americans received "fair severance packages commensurate with their years of service," she added.

- At New York Life, three hundred layoffs were part of a $1 billion plan to modernize the insurance giant's financial and information technology. The American employees found out about the cuts only by accident, when managers working for a consultant in India mistakenly sent out a mass email with the full outsourcing plan. New York Life employees were surprised to hear that Indian workers had already been in training for several weeks to replace them and would soon be taking their jobs back to India. One accountant said a worker from India sat by his desk and made an exact digital record of his keystrokes, then transmitted the data each night to India, where workers copied his every task. "We know there will be pain along the way," said New York Life senior vice president William Werfelman, who added that the cuts and some innovative technology would allow the company to expand rapidly in other areas.

- At Southern California Edison, the West Coast's largest utility, data employees were upset to hear about a four-hundred-person layoff. But the disappointment turned to something "beyond furious," one worker said, when he and his colleagues discovered they were being replaced by H-1B "guest workers" from India. And not only that. Some of the outgoing Americans were asked to train their replacements. A "transition effort," the process was called. One employee was quoted as saying: "They are bringing in people with a couple of years' experience to replace us and then we have to train them. It's demoralizing and in a way I kind of felt betrayed by the company."

LAND OF IMMIGRANTS AND FREE TRADE

America is a nation of immigrants. We have a glorious tradition of welcoming people from around the world. Our country has been enriched—actually, it's been defined—by the constant influx from abroad. That's what the Statue of Liberty is all about and how our country has learned to replenish itself. Historically, we have not hidden behind high walls. Almost all our families came from somewhere else, including mine. The new ones keep coming for the same reasons most of our ancestors did—for the opportunity to better support themselves and their families. And they arrive with a powerful hope in their hearts—that with hard work and luck they too can capture a share of the legendary American Dream.

I'm not opposed to that any more than I'm opposed to the concept of free trade, as long as it's done appropriately. We're not a protectionist nation. We all use imported goods. Free and robust trade, as long as it's fair trade, has the potential to improve everyone's quality of life. But still, I believe most Americans are tired of having their hopes raised and then dashed by all the soaring promises of inter-nationalism. From NAFTA to GATT to the WTO to H-1B, it's been one, long national disappointment: Don't you feel like you've seen this movie before? Bright promise, grim results. Our generous tra-ditions should not be a license for others to pick our pockets in the name of openness, yet that's what keeps happening over and over again. These H-1B visas, nice as they sound in theory, have turned out to be just the latest in a long line of examples of U.S. workers get-ting squeezed.

I understand business executives working strenuously to push their costs down. We all do that. Business isn't a charity. It's a profit-seeking enterprise. Our companies are not jobs programs for worthy Americans. I get all that. And I am always sympathetic to the idea of fair competition and foreign workers bettering themselves. If foreign companies or foreign labor recruiters think they can really do the job better than our people can—let them try to compete, I say. But what's happening here just isn't right. They are here under false pretenses. We follow the law. While we open our doors to others, we also have to look out for fellow Americans. The more you learn about situations like this, the more you see how tilted the field of competition has become. If our people don't win this or that competition, that's fine in a fair fight. But it's often because they were never given a fair chance to compete for it. As American business leaders, don't we owe American workers a fair fight?

THEIR SIDE OF THE STORY

I know the other side of this. I know what companies like Toys "R" Us usually say. "Everyone else is doing it. We need the savings.

To compete we have to do it, too. We're getting a better deal from TCS and their 'guest' accountants."

Do two wrongs make a right? I hear companies that send their call centers, billing departments, and other back-office functions overseas, then quickly turn around and bring them back to America. Those overseas bargains weren't such bargains after all. They were cheap, in every sense of the word. Let's be real here. If the Indian accountants are so darn brilliant, why do they have to come to New Jersey to learn how to do the jobs?

And what about the concept of fair play? Do you think in your wildest imagination, India, or for that matter any other nation, would ever do the same for us? Train our people to snatch their jobs from them? Invite a crew of American workers to Bangalore to learn the Indian worker's moves? We're back to the factory owner I met with in Hong Kong who told me he'd never met anyone as greedy or as naïve as the Americans.

If we continue to permit the rampant use of H-1B visas to replace American workers, it's as if we have all thrown in the towel. It's like we aren't willing to educate our workforce to do anything and everything that needs to be done. We're saying that American workers are too lazy or too incompetent or too incapable of improvement to justify keeping those jobs here at home.

This isn't the best of America. It is not all we are capable of. What Toys "R" Us and the others did—that's not even giving the American employees a chance. They didn't ask, "Can you improve? We need you to improve. Or we need to get this job done more efficiently. We'd like your help." This was just, "Here are your replacements. Show them what to do. Goodbye."

You know what a U.S. marine would think of that. When you go into the Marine Corps, one of the core values is never leave a fellow marine behind. If he's wounded, even if he's dead, the same ethic applies. Drag your buddy out with you. American business could use a strong dose of that same esprit de corps. If we are going to compete globally now, if we are going to pay higher wages, provide better benefits, offer a safer workplace, have a cleaner environment—all the things America stands for and tries to achieve—if we are going to be the country that everyone wants to live in, if we have all these benefits, we'd better have the most cohesive teams out there.

I cannot imagine ever doing anything like what these H-1B outsourcers have done. How about the people who haven't been replaced, who still have their jobs? How do they respond? How do they feel about the management of their company at that point? How comfortable are they working with a company that will do that to other employees? Do you think they will be delivering their best possible performance if they don't trust the people they are working for? Or do you think they'll be sneaking around behind their employer's back, trying to find a new job as soon as possible?

Nothing is more painful in business than the need to lay off employees. Still, no company, certainly not ours, can ever say unequivocally, "We will never have layoffs, no matter what." But you can say this: "We will do everything we can do avoid it. But should we need to have layoffs, we'll do it as humanely as possible. We'll try to find other places in the company for people who are displaced. We'll offer severance payments and give people as much notice as we possibly can."

We owe our workers at least that much.

This is partly a matter of human decency. These are loyal employees. We have asked them to do a job, and they have done it. They held up their end of the employment bargain. We are the ones who have been unable to hold up ours. But it's also a matter of living up to what we believe and protecting the company culture for those who remain.

WHEN YOU HAVE TO

Should a round of layoffs ever be necessary, there is a right and wrong way to handle it, even for a company like Toys "R" Us. Do it the right way! If their executives really had to squeeze large savings out of the accounting department, why not call those sixty-seven people in and begin a dialogue, ideally before the moment of crisis has arrived? Make it a conversation, not a summary execution. Say, "Guys, we have to compete. We have to get better and faster. We have to make fewer mistakes. We might even need to eliminate some jobs in the department. But let's all work together and figure out how we can get this done."

I know American workers. I know what they are capable of. It's far more than the cynics give them credit for. American workers are especially loath to walk away from a challenge, especially if they are asked to help solve it. Especially if they have respect and trust for the people who are leading them. It's management's responsibility to earn that trust.

Continue the conversation in this focused but cooperative vein. Say, "We'd rather not cut positions in the department, but if we have to, the first thing we will do is absorb as many of those people as we can in other parts of our company. We won't cut anyone's wages. We won't send anyone to the sidewalk. But we have to make some changes in order to compete more effectively and keep this organization profitable and alive. We've got to make this a better organization. We need your help."

I would hate to ever have that conversation at Vaughan-Bassett—

desperately hate to. But if circumstances required it, I do believe our people would step up and help us figure it out. We'd really be taking Helen and her colleagues in the finishing room up on their kind offer. We have that history together. We have that level of trust.

It is so important to speak openly with your people, especially when pain is on the way. Everyone today understands the harsh reality of the workplace. Everyone knows how ruthless competition can be. Believe me, people will cooperate if you give them the chance. Bringing them into the conversation as early as possible is always the way to go. Build on the team you have already developed. It will enhance the group cohesion. Do what is necessary to compete even in the most difficult of times.

But if cuts ultimately have to be made, do everything as cleanly, openly, and humanely as you can.

- Let everyone know what is happening.
- At every step of the way, explain why.
- Offer as many alternatives as possible.
- Invite the employees to suggest cost-cutting options of their own.
- Weigh those suggestions seriously.
- Give people plenty of notice.
- Find other places in the company to absorb the people who are cut.
- Provide sufficient training for them to thrive in their new positions.
- Let them know how much you appreciate their special sacrifice and what an important part of the team they remain.
- Help them succeed in their new roles.

- If at all possible, give them a route back should their old positions return.

Isn't that a company you'd want to work for? Isn't that an organization you'd still feel loyal to? Who can ask more than that from an employer?

That doesn't mean all pain can be eliminated. It doesn't mean a business has been turned into a charity. What it means is two things: We owe our best efforts to the people who have given their best efforts to us, and we see the value in preserving the culture of the organization once any necessary trims are made. Don't tell me those people won't give their all in the weeks and months to come.

You treat people like human beings, not entries on a ledger or just another budget line. It comes down to that in the end. Business is a people business, whatever business you are in.

Sit down with your people and say to them, "We've got a problem here. Let's see if we can solve it together." Some of those financial people, all they do is look at numbers. They forget. Behind every number is a person trying to succeed. That's what we used to do in this country—give people a chance to succeed.

THE LEADER'S ACTION PLAN: CHAPTER 11

DOING IT

FIRST, TRY TO AVOID IT. Cutting employees is a drastic step that you should undertake only when absolutely necessary. Start by looking for another way. Can you fill the hole with higher revenues, not lower expenses? Are there new efficiencies you haven't yet discovered? Is there some other fat you can possibly cut? Is there technology you can purchase that will give you an edge? Truly exhaust those options before taking out the ax.

WHEN CUTS ARE LOOMING, TALK TO YOUR PEOPLE BEFORE IT'S TOO LATE. No one knows the business better than they do. They may well have valuable insights and alternate ideas. Share the numbers. Lay out the issues. Listen to everyone's ideas. Weigh them. Try them. This has two benefits. Your employees might suggest something you haven't thought of, and even if their input doesn't solve the problem, they'll accept cuts better knowing that you tried to save their jobs.

DO IT HUMANELY. Give notice. Offer transfers. Pay for training. Let your people know their sacrifice is appreciated. Help them succeed wherever they are headed next. Give them a route back. There are two reasons to make cuts humanely: It's the right thing to do, and it sends a message to everyone who remains. This is an organization you can still have pride in.

TREAT THE BAD NEWS AS TEMPORARY. There's a tendency, when pain is inflicted, to feel like pain is the new way of life. This needn't be true, and it won't be if the organization springs sufficiently ahead. Expand your ambitions, don't contract them. Let the bad news serve as a jolt of energy. Don't accept the notion of a long, slow slide. Bring the old people back as quickly as possible. This can be a breather, and not the end.

Chapter 12

Buy American

No single shift in consumer behavior will bring more improvement to the U.S. economy than this—everyday people buying more American products. It requires no act of Congress and no executive order by the president. It will slash unemployment and increase tax revenues. It will reduce the budget deficit and improve the trade imbalance. It requires no new regulations or tax increases. Just buy American when you can. The impact of that one change in consumer behavior will be enormous.

I t starts by asking.

The next time you walk into a store, ask the salesperson, "Do you have anything that's made in our country?"

Just ask!

"Can you show me something that was manufactured in the USA?"

If you want to help keep jobs here, if you want to make sure the next generation has the opportunities that previous generations have enjoyed, the number-one thing you can do right now is to ask. Let retailers know you are concerned about where their products come from. Whether it's a watch or a bottle of whiskey, a pair of shoes or chest of drawers, let the people at the store know that this makes a difference to you. Say, "I like to buy American when I can."

Just ask. These are powerful words.

When I say *American,* by the way, I don't mean *North* American. Canada and Mexico will just have to fend for themselves on this one. I am talking about the *United States* of America, the country that has given so much to us and deserves a little more support in return.

Even if you can't afford to buy, you can afford to ask. This is so important, let me say it again. Even if you can't afford to buy, you can afford to ask. Believe me, retailers will pick up on this if people keep asking. Store owners will make it their business to stock American-made products.

If the store clerk says, "No, we don't have anything that's American-made," follow up nicely with "Why not?" If American-made products are available and the store doesn't give its customers that choice—well, that tells you something, doesn't it? If no such products exist—if the factories that used to make the item have all moved overseas—then that reminds everyone how much more work we have to do.

Either way, I promise you the salesperson or the clerk or the cashier will pass your question on to the manager or the owner or the buyers or whoever's deciding what is stocked on those shelves. Every retailer wants to stock what customers want to buy. If that means U.S.-made products, they will move heaven and earth to find a way.

Any time our nation's products are in the market, we should have a chance to buy them. We as American consumers hold a huge amount of power in our hands. We should be prepared to use it by buying competitive domestic goods. Not suffering. Not hurting ourselves. Not denying our families anything. Just being aware of the issue and, when it makes sense, trying to buy products made by our fellow countrymen. American manufacturers don't need special favors. We don't need the government to mandate buy-American affirmative action. What we need is access to the market and a level playing field.

When that happens, we do just fine.

I'm not interested in making anyone feel guilty or telling anyone, "You're terrible if you don't buy American." I don't believe that. If you don't want to buy the American product, that's absolutely your choice. American companies have to compete for your business just like everyone else does. But give customers the option. Let them know where the product comes from. "Made in China."

"Made in India." "Made in the USA." Don't hide that. Put it out there. Then let the customer decide.

I especially love when people request American products in a furniture store, and not only because it tends to generate sales for Vaughan-Bassett—though, sure, that's an added bonus for us. "Is this dining room suite made in America? Where is this entertainment center manufactured?" That's music to my ears. "This occasional table?" Unfortunately, with occasional tables, the answer is almost always someplace else. Hardly anyone is building occasional in America anymore. Maybe that's an opportunity for someone.

One thing we've discovered at Vaughan-Bassett: The more American-made products are highlighted with consumers, the better those products sell. The first step to getting people to buy American is letting them know something is American-made. That's why we love it when retailers feature our furniture in special made-in-America galleries.

In February 2015, Brown Squirrel Furniture in Knoxville, Tennessee, opened a dynamic made-in-America gallery. Vaughan-Bassett bedroom suites are featured prominently. Customers see the furniture and like it. They recognize the value, style, and workmanship. The fact that it's made in America is an added selling point. They like hearing that. Customers buy a lot more of our furniture than they had before, and Brown Squirrel has the sales figures to prove it.

Brown Squirrel wasn't the first retailer to do this. Grand Home Furnishings in Roanoke, Virginia, has had a made-in-America wood-furniture gallery since July 2012. Others have been opening them as well. Almost without exception, it's an approach that's connected well with customers. It's a selling strategy I hope is becoming a national trend. It's just another example of Americans eager to buy American—when they have the opportunity and the information to do so.

I treasure the dealer who says, "We buy everything we can in America and let the customer know where the products come from." Really, that's all I ask. It doesn't mean the whole store will be filled with American products, but at least customers are given that choice. I have great confidence in American workers and American companies. Give us a shot at the business. We'll find ways to compete effectively and produce goods people find attractive. We've proven it at Vaughan-Bassett. They've proven it in Detroit. Others are proving it elsewhere every day. I have no doubt we will get a healthy share, hopefully more than a healthy share.

That's the kind of retailer I want to support, one who offers a good choice of products, one who supports the country, one who boosts the economy, one who helps save jobs. That retailer is also helping his own business by creating the next wave of customers for that store and others, people with money in their pockets from an increasingly robust economy, who will soon be in the market to buy. It's a beautiful thing—the circle of a healthy economy.

Often, when I give a speech, someone will stand up during the question-and-answer time and ask, "What can *I* do to help? I'm just one person. I'm not a politician. I'm not a major retailer or a large manufacturer or a Washington regulator. What can one person possibly do to support American manufacturing and save American jobs?"

For a long time, I wasn't sure how to answer that question. But I was invited to speak to the Woman's Club of Richmond, a well-established group of highly engaged women in Virginia's capital city. My sister, Jane Bassett Spilman, is a member and agreed to introduce me. Besides saying I'm her brother, she used one phrase several times in her introduction. She spoke of "the power of one." How one company had made a difference. How one leader can have an outsize impact. How one person really can change the world.

I love that concept, "the power of one." It can be extraordinary. That day, Jane reminded me of the power all of us hold in our hearts and our hands. And when a woman stood and asked that familiar question—"what can one person possibly do?"—this time I had an answer for her.

"Just ask.

"Buy American when you can.

"If you can't, just ask.

"You have no idea how much power one person has."

Things change when a customer walks into a store and asks, "What do you have that's made in America?"

Just ask!

It's just one person—an executive, an employee, a customer—making all the difference in the world. That's the power of one.

WHERE'S THE LINE?

I am not against foreign imports coming into the country. How could I be? I love the made-in-Scotland game of golf, and as has already been established, I enjoy the occasional glass of French wine. I appreciate a bargain as much as anyone does. Sometimes, with some products, foreign manufacturers just do a better job. We competed. They competed. They won. It may be—just to pick a product more or less at random—that China does a better job of mass-producing wood screws than America does. God bless 'em. Maybe that's not the terrain for us to compete on. We'll just have to find some other products to make better than they do, and we certainly can.

Do you have more confidence in a product made in this country than in a product made elsewhere? It depends on what the product is, right? Japanese cars used to be a joke. Gradually, their quality has improved to the point that they're some of the best cars in the world. Public confidence skyrocketed, even in America—and deservedly so.

Boeing, the aerospace giant, is now building aircraft in China in partnership with AVIC, Aviation Industries Corporation of China. Over time, it's possible people will come to have confidence in Chinese-made aircraft. Personally, I'm not there yet. I still have more confidence in a Boeing plane out of Seattle or South Carolina than one from the Binhai New Area of Tianjin. I certainly feel more secure on a major Western airline than I do on some foreign carriers.

The last time I flew to St. Petersburg, Russia, I took a British Airways flight to London. I was planning to spend a night near Heathrow Airport before flying out the next day to St. Petersburg. "Mr. Bassett," the British customs officer said to me as I was leaving Terminal Three, "I see you're departing tomorrow for St. Petersburg."

"I am," I said.

"And you're staying in our fair city just for tonight?"

"I am."

He looked at me as if this seemed odd to him. "Do you realize you flew from New York?"

"Yes."

"Do you know you can get a direct flight from New York to St. Petersburg?"

"I know," I said.

It was obvious that he considered my behavior unusual, if not downright suspicious.

"Would you explain to me why you're doing what you're doing?"

"May I ask you a question?" I replied.

"What?" he asked.

"Do *you* want to fly Aeroflot?"

The customs agent smiled. "Good answer," he said. "Enjoy your stay. Come back soon."

You may feel differently, and these are the kinds of questions shrewd consumers naturally ask. They assess the evidence before them. They gauge their own comfort and taste. They consider parallel facts.

There are many, many products that Americans do—and can— make better than manufacturers anywhere. Movies and television shows. A wide range of agricultural products. Trucks and automobiles. Energy products. I'd certainly put wood bedroom suites on that list.

Frankly, this shouldn't be all that tough a sell. Americans want to buy American. Every poll shows this is true. In survey after survey, upwards of 80 percent of Americans readily say they believe in buying American products—and for some of the same reasons I do. Trusted brand names. High-quality products. Helping the economy. Saving American jobs. Defunding inhumane practices in foreign factories. One other thing the pollsters have found: A tie usually goes to the domestic manufacturer—even a near-tie. If the American product and the imported product are both being sold for $11.99, most people will buy American. They'll probably do the same if the domestic product is $12.09. But if the American-made item is $16.99 compared to $11.99, most American consumers will say "no thanks" to that.

Clearly, there is a line, but it's a wavy one. It's hard to come up with a precise percentage that applies every time. Of course, that hasn't stopped researchers from trying, and they've assembled some useful hints. In a recent survey by the Boston Consulting Group, more than 60 percent said they would buy American clothes and appliances even if those items cost 10 percent more than the imported brands. More than 25 percent said they would pay at least an extra 20 percent. Here's the real kicker: The consultants found that more than 60 percent of Chinese respondents said they would buy the American-made version over the Chinese even if it cost more.

They should know, right?

BUY AND BUY, THE MOST COMPELLING CASE EVER

My theory is that a lot of Americans just haven't studied this issue. At the same time, many retailers have gotten comfortable selling imported products and have chosen not to rock the boat. Our challenge, therefore, is to get people thinking and talking about the importance of buying American. When they do, American companies and American consumers almost inevitably win. We have great stories to tell, great products to offer, and the added bonus of helping to rescue a languishing U.S. economy. Not a bad result for a quick trip to the store.

The case for buying American is a powerful one: Absorb it. Mention it as often as you can. Repeat it to friends, family, and coworkers every chance you get. Once people hear why they should be buying American products, it makes them think, and they almost always agree.

- **Buying American creates American jobs.** Even a little goes a long way. There are many methods for counting this. According to a recent ABC News analysis, if everyone in America spent an extra $3.33 on U.S.-made products each year, it would produce an extra 10,000 jobs. If every builder used 5 percent more American-made materials, that would create 220,000 jobs. However you count it, there's no getting around the basic connection between purchasing American products and creating American jobs: The more we buy American-made products, the more Americans will be employed—supporting families, reviving communities, teaching skills, passing on a legacy everyone can be proud of. If you think the unemployment is too low, keep buying foreign products. If you think it's too high, look for the "Made in the USA" tag.

- **Buying American releases the multiplier effect.** Think of our domestic economy as a giant echo chamber. Anything good that happens is repeated several times over. And it's exactly the same with anything bad. That's the "multiplier effect." Economists say that every dollar spent on American goods or services multiplies an average of seven times. Think about what happens if you buy a single American-made towel, assuming you can find one. From the four dollars you just spent, the mill owner pays the line worker. The line worker can hire a babysitter and go out to dinner on Saturday night. That helps the café owner pay the waitress, who can now afford to get her car repaired by the local mechanic, who can now— you get the idea. That single towel purchase has only begun to multiply. None of that would have happened if that single American consumer bought a Pakistani towel. The experts say that every manufacturing job held by an American spins off another 5 to 8 American jobs.

- **Buying American recycles consumer dollars through the economy.** Just as workers' salaries do, consumer spending on American products propels the economy. It hires more workers. It pays suppliers, suppliers who can then buy American and in turn hire more Americans. It generates tax revenues. It trains a new generation of workers. It fuels a cycle that keeps on giving, over and over. The only dead dollars are the ones that leave the country, where they may fuel some foreign economy but do almost no good for us in America.

- **Buying American makes the planet healthier.** U.S. manufacturers are heavily regulated, forbidden to pollute the air, spoil the rivers, emit radiation, and harm the earth in an assortment of other ways. We have some of the strictest environmental laws in the world. Our toughest foreign competitors have almost none. Many U.S. companies, ours included, go well beyond what the law requires, considering themselves genuine stewards of the earth. At Vaughan-Bassett, we have what we call our 1-4-1 Program. For every tree we use to make furniture, we buy a fresh seedling to be planted as a replacement—literally 1-4-1. Since 2007, we inform the Virginia Department of Forestry how much oak, cherry, pine, maple, poplar, and other varieties we use each year, and they tell us how many trees will replace that. We purchase the seedlings. The state foresters give the baby trees to individuals, community organizations, nonprofit groups, clubs, and schools, who plant them in specific locales across the state. So far, the 1-4-1 program has distributed 1.3 million seedlings, helping Virginia maintain a key part of its natural beauty. This is sustainability at its best, and I believe our program is unique. Because of that and other similar efforts, the carbon footprint of most American factories, to use one current measure, is a tiny fraction of what most foreign manufacturing facilities record. The real threat of climate change, environmentalists keep pointing out, comes from industrial China, India, and other foreign manufacturers. Before you complain about the U.S. pollution, get a lungful of Beijing, Mexico City, or Jakarta. If you care about the oceans, the wetlands, the skies, and the forests, support manufacturers that share your concerns. It's our barely regulated foreign competitors who are dumping toxic chemicals, spewing untreated carbons, and reporting none of it to anyone. And do you have any idea how much petroleum is burned every year to ship all those products to America?

- **Buying American keeps workers safe.** America has some of the toughest worker-protection laws in the world. Unfortunately, many of the countries with the lowest-cost production treat their people the worst. Starvation wages. Exploitation of children. Unsafe working conditions and unspeakable abuses of various sorts. How do you think they can afford to make the stuff so cheaply? That's the system American consumers are often supporting when purchasing foreign goods. With American-made products, we can be confident that a certain standard of law and human decency is maintained.

- **Buying American promotes research and development.** Spending money on U.S.-made goods helps to create new and improved products everyone can trust. It's just a fact: The vast majority of creative development happens right here in America. Our corporations support it. Our government encourages it. Our consumers appreciate it. But that intense R&D, which can take years or decades to pay for itself, ultimately depends on the flow of consumer dollars once those products are sold. If people buy more American products, America will create something newer, safer, and better every time.

- **Buying American helps to end poverty and dependence at home.** The kinds of jobs that have been lost are just the kinds of jobs America now needs most. Jobs for hard-working people. Jobs for people without advanced degrees and highly specialized skills. Jobs that are stable, offer benefits, and tend to be secure. Jobs that pull someone out of poverty, off welfare, up from food stamps, and into the solid working, middle class. Jobs that will support American families. Our nation used to be loaded with jobs like those in the industrial heartland, in the Rust Belt, in the large northern cities, across the South and the West. Those are the jobs that were lost as American industry was battered. Those are the jobs that buying American can help to bring back.

- **Buying American puts trustworthy products into American homes.** Fewer dangerous toys. Fewer toxic paint chips. Fewer mold-producing building materials. Fewer deadly baby cribs. It isn't that American-made products are always perfect. A few bad ones do sometimes slip through. But we have a fully integrated system in place, developed over decades, to protect consumer safety. It includes state and federal regulations, the constant threat of lawsuits, and the good intentions of most American businesspeople, who have to face their customers every day. All that has come together to give us the most tested, the most screened, and ultimately the most safe products in the world.

GARBAGE IN, GARBAGE IN

Sometimes, cheap foreign products aren't quite the bargains they appear to be. They may be cheap for a reason. Just ask the companies that have been caught up in massive product recalls—or the angry customers who've returned to confront them. In one recent year, foreign manufacturers produced 8 of every 10 products recalled by the U.S. Consumer Product Safety Commission, according to an analysis by the American Association for Justice, a national trial lawyers group. It seems to be a trend.

Toxic flooring: After a scathing investigation by CBS's *60 Minutes* found high levels of formaldehyde in 2015, Lumber Liquidators suspended all sales of laminate flooring made in China. Company executives insisted the flooring was safe but conceded "mounting industry concerns relating to laminate products sourced from China." Really, what choice did they have? They'd already sent out 26,000 testing kits to customers. One hundred and three class-action lawsuits had been filed. The Consumer Product Safety Commission was investigating, and the Department of Justice was threatening criminal charges. Oh, and the company's stock price had tumbled 47 percent.

- **Counterfeit breathing masks:** The air in Beijing is so polluted these days, Chinese officials have declared a health emergency air pollution red alert. This serious warning came as more and more of their citizens are refusing to go outside without breathing masks. But are the masks themselves toxic? Customs authorities in Shanghai seized 120,000 counterfeit 3M masks, saying the fakes posed special dangers of their own. Chinese social media erupted in angry debate: Were the shoddy masks being exported to other countries or intended for use at home? And which was worse?

- **Radioactive drywall:** In 2006, just as the U.S. housing market was exploding, the demand for drywall outpaced what domestic suppliers could produce. China eagerly stepped in. But soon homeowners were complaining that the Chinese drywall was causing foul odors. Mirrors were mysteriously corroding. Electrical outlets kept shorting out. After a quick investigation, experts found the cause— phosphogypsum, a radioactive material also known to cause lung cancer, was present at dangerous levels in the Chinese drywall. Huge lawsuits were filed. Some still haven't been settled. Thousands of houses, including many renovations after Hurricane Katrina, had to be rebuilt from the studs. The entire U.S. drywall industry was thrown into upheaval and has yet to fully recover.

- **Tainted toys:** Hardly any mass-market toys are made in America anymore. They almost all come from China. This has meant a rash of recalls, pullbacks, and class-action lawsuits over the safety of these Chinese-made toys. In one recent year, 467 different types of China-made toys—including some components of the hugely popular Thomas & Friends wooden train sets—were recalled over lead paint concerns. That paint, long banned in the United States as a cause of brain damage in children, was also found on 463,000 Mattel-branded die-cast toys, 175,000 Marvel Curious George dolls, and 51,000 Dolgencorp children's sunglasses. Soon after that, Cracker Barrel, McDonald's, and other fast-food restaurants recalled Chinese-made children's-meal giveaway toys over safety concerns.

There are many, many other examples, from tainted toothpaste to poison pet food to seafood that could soon be glowing in the dark. It would be totally unfair to suggest that all or most foreign products are inferior. At the same time, American consumers can't afford to be naïve.

SAVE MONEY, BUY AMERICAN

Sam Walton believed in buying and selling American. He put American flags all over his Wal-Mart stores and took great pride in offering products that were made by American workers in American factories and sold to American customers hungry for an attractive low price. He loved America and had much to be thankful for. He had, after all, turned a single dime store in Arkansas cotton country into the largest retailer on earth. He even called his autobiography *Made in America,* a reference to his own life and to the products he so proudly sold.

So, yes, it's ironic—sadly ironic—that Wal-Mart became such a voracious customer of imported goods. The company's massive volume and legendarily tough negotiating style really helped to undermine the U.S. manufacturing sector and laid a pathway into America for bottom-feeding plants in China, India, Mexico, and other low-wage countries around the world. In a relentless push for rock-bottom prices, Wal-Mart buyers often find lowest of the low overseas. In Sam Walton's later years—and especially since his death in 1992—the vast majority of the items on Wal-Mart's shelves might as well have been slapped with a tag that reads, "Not Made in America." It's hard to know exactly how the company's founder would have felt about that—"There is only one boss," he famously said, "the customer"—and the customers undeniably flocked to the lower prices.

I went to Wal-Mart near my home to buy some new socks. Yes, I shop at Wal-Mart sometimes. I won't pretend otherwise. The Hanes socks I found were perfectly nice socks and undeniably well priced. I think they came to about $1.05 a pair. Wal-Mart probably paid fifty cents a pair. It doesn't take an MBA to know where those socks came from—and it wasn't North Carolina. "Made in El Salvador," the small tag said.

I should have asked the clerk what else they had in the sock aisle. "Any USA-made products?" I'm kicking myself for not doing that, though I can't predict how fruitful that would have been this time. The hosiery industry has been hit as hard as wood furniture has, maybe harder. And things haven't improved much for them. The latest figures I saw said imports account for more than 80 percent of the socks and pantyhose sold in America, according to the American Apparel & Footwear Association. U.S. employment in the industry is less than a quarter of what it was fifteen years earlier. The U.S. sock-making industry has been so badly devastated by imports that the main trade group, the Hosiery Association, disbanded in 2013.

But all is not hopeless at Wal-Mart, any more than it's hopeless for America or its struggling workers and domestic manufacturers.

WAL-MART REDISCOVERS ITS ROOTS

Maybe Sam Walton called down from heaven. Maybe the current Wal-Mart executives got tired of the bad PR. Or maybe someone was rereading the old man's autobiography. Whatever the explanation, the giant retailer seems to have gotten religion on the benefits of American-made products—or at least a tentative recognition that too much importing can actually be considered a sin.

In 2013, Wal-Mart pledged publicly to buy an extra $250 billion in U.S.-made products over the next decade. That's a big number, even for a company this massive. The announcement generated an immediate burst of positive publicity—and some practical questions about how the rapid expansion would actually occur. Some Wal-Mart suppliers warned that it wouldn't be as easy as just flipping on a switch. The challenges included too few American factories still in operation and a too-shallow pool of experienced workers to staff the ones we had left, let alone the new ones needed to meet the fresh wave of the huge retailer's product demand.

"A lot of the tribal knowledge and skill sets are gone because the humans who used to do that work have either retired or died," Kim Kelley, CEO of Hampton Products International, a maker of locks, lighting, and other household wares, told an interviewer. His California-based company, which began selling Asian-made products to Wal-Mart in the 1990s, took up the domestic challenge nonetheless.

To spur the effort along, Wal-Mart held supplier summits in Denver and Orlando. The company called in economic development officials from states eager to encourage new factories. The company also held an "open call" at its Bentonville, Arkansas, headquarters for any U.S. suppliers who wanted to pitch their business.

But $250 billion is $250 billion, and as you might imagine, American companies are finding a way. Once they get up and running—and shake the cobwebs off—more and more of them are earning a place for their American-made products on Wal-Mart's shelves. It's far too little and far too late to predict a sweeping rebirth of American manufacturing, but it's a start, and here's hoping the idea picks up steam.

Wal-Mart execs say customers can now walk into a store or hop on the website and buy lightbulbs, towels, curtains, and flat-screen TVs, all made in America.

The flat screens are made in Winnsboro, South Carolina, by Element Electronics. Until the Wal-Mart push, Element made all its TVs in Asia and had failed to get Wal-Mart to stock them.

"We began to think about what we could do differently," said CEO Mike O'Shaughnessy. "Well, one of the things we could do differently is to make our TVs at home."

Six months later, the company opened a 315,000-square-foot plant in South Carolina, hiring five hundred local employees. The plant has six assembly lines making 32-, 40-, and 50-inch TVs. They are now for sale in more than four thousand Wal-Mart stores.

Many of the parts still come from overseas. But that too could change over time. "Longer term," the CEO said, "the more success we have procuring our parts domestically, the better off we expect to be."

It's the story of American manufacturing, told all over again.

It's a spirit that extends far beyond one new TV maker in South Carolina. It's an attitude Americans have in abundance and still need more of. Has the time come to fall in love with America again? Only you can answer that question. Just ask!

THE LEADER'S ACTION PLAN: CHAPTER 12

BORN, MADE, STAYED

Be for the home team. Be conscious of the power of your American consumer dollars, whether you are a businessperson or not. The best way to grow American employment is to purchase products and services that are American made. Buying American really can create jobs, build communities, change our country, and help an awful lot of people get through their lives. That's what jobs do, and we could use more of them.

Buy American when you can. I know, it isn't always easy. Some products are hardly made here anymore. And retailers can be cagey about where things come from. But the good news is that American manufacturers have never been more talented and more efficient than they are right now. Some wonderful products are made in America. Buying American isn't a matter of sacrificing on price or quality. It's a chance to enjoy first-rate goods.

Just ask. "What do you have that's made in America?" When stores stock American goods, praise them for that. When they don't, ask, "Why not?" Just asking can change everything. It tells the retailers that this is something customers care about. It makes businesspeople think. It reminds everyone that the nation has to focus on competition. It says, "Our best days are still ahead."

You are powerful. You may be just one, but that one is hugely powerful. It's your money. You have a right to decide how it is spent. Spending it on U.S.-made products has many benefits. You'll be getting good stuff. You'll be spurring the economy. You'll be creating the next generation of American consumer—people with jobs spend money—and the next generation of American goods. That's achieving a lot from a simple trip to the store.

Chapter 13

Will It Ever Return

A lot of people in our industry used to call me Don Quixote. "There's Bassett," they'd say, "the Man from La Mancha, fighting windmills again." In the past few years, I've had a few of them pull me aside and say, "You are right. We should have done something. We shouldn't have just shut down everything." When people say, "We can't," I instinctively think, Oh, yes we can. Just watch. Not in every instance. Not in the face of irrefutable evidence. Not always. But I've never been one for premature surrender. There's always time for that later on. But guys, let's not turn our backs on this country. Let's keep fighting now. The best really could be yet to come.

Will it ever return?

I am constantly asked that question—by friends, employees, colleagues, competitors, folks I see at church on Sunday morning, and others who stop me in the hardware store on Saturday afternoon. They know the role our company has played saving American jobs, and they want to hear my perspective. Every time I travel, I am asked the same thing.

"John," people say, "will American manufacturing ever come back again?"

Some people are highly skeptical of the prospects. They say: "Just get used to it. America has lost this battle. We can't compete in the global market anymore. Leave manufacturing to low-wage factories in second-tier countries. We should focus on finance and service and making blockbuster Hollywood films."

Others, like me, aren't ready to throw in the towel. We say: "Give us the opportunity. We will compete—and win!"

Clearly, this is a topic that provokes some sharply divided outlooks, but we don't all have to be on different sides. First, just about everyone wants American manufacturing to thrive again. "America should make things again," people are constantly saying, and I know they mean it. They understand: If all we do is provide services to each other and move money around, at some point we will be incapable of making anything at all. That's a kind of dependency that just doesn't say America.

Manufacturing is such a significant part of our country's heritage. From the late 1700s, when Samuel Slater built America's first factory for making cotton textiles, to Henry Ford and forward, the mass production of goods in American factories has been a driving force of the U.S. economy. Those businesses created millions and millions of jobs and helped to establish the American middle class. Along with the American military, the products those factories produced helped to define our nation to the world. From clothes to cars, from televisions to appliances—certainly add furniture to that potent lineup—making and marketing stuff kept America growing and affluent through the twentieth century and into the twenty-first. Watching that engine sputter and at times run out of gas has been unnerving for many Americans, deeply painful for some.

And sputter it has.

Dozens of other countries are in the game now. Some of them have spent quite a few years now kicking our butts. Too many products once made in places like Galax, Virginia, and Detroit, Michigan, are rolling out of factories in nations that barely had factories a generation or two ago. At this point, the trend is too large for anyone to ignore. *We've lost over 7 million manufacturing jobs since 1979. That's 37 percent of everyone who once built things. Since 2002 we've lost more factory jobs than at any time in U.S. history. At one time more than 1 in 4 Americans worked in a manufacturing business. Today, fewer than 9 percent of American men and women work on or near a production line.* And the same forces that snatched away those factory jobs are now taking a toll on technology, finance, telecommunications, and other fields America once unquestionably dominated.

Of course, I take all this personally. How could I not? When you work in an industry like furniture and live in America's traditional furniture belt, you come face-to-face with these changes every time you step out of the house. In the past few years, a lot more companies around here have been closing factories than opening them. Our company stands out not because we are so phenomenally successful or because we are sparking such a huge trend in American furniture making—but because we are here. And that in itself is extraordinary. Despite all that was stacked against us, we have survived and we aim to be here for a good, long time.

Manufacturing isn't dead in America, not by a long shot, and Vaughan-Bassett isn't the only company keeping it alive. We have a number of allies today and are constantly seeking more—in furniture making and in other industries as well. It's important to point out that, despite the declines, manufacturing is still a significant part of the U.S. economy, even now. It adds up to more than $2 trillion a year, according to the latest government figures, a number that's been rising steadily since 2009. Let me say that again: a number that's been rising steadily since 2009, despite fewer employees and fewer factories. There are some genuine signs that American manufacturing really may be inching back.

As I look across the landscape today, I see reasons for this hopeful trend. All are worth applauding.

- **Wages are rising across the developing world.** Once people get a taste of the fruits of capitalism—money in their pockets! a fair shot at the middle class!—it's hard to tell them they should work for slave wages again. Nowhere is this more true than in China. Since 2001, the hourly pay of Chinese factory workers has gone up an average of 12 percent a year. The yuan, China's heavily weighted national currency, has been at an all-time high, putting further pressure on domestic costs. This doesn't mean that China is losing its commanding position as a manufacturing center, but it does reduce one of the country's chief advantages in competing against us. As happens almost everywhere, rising domestic wages has only planted a craving for more. Once lifted, they are damn near impossible to roll back.

- **The red-hot Asian economies are finally slowing down.** Heavy debts, a property slump, greater skepticism abroad—these are tough economic times across Asia. The issues are severe enough that they've even been rattling the U.S. stock market. China, Japan, and South Korea—the region's big three economies—have all had to trim their high-flying expectations. No one's saying their economies are crashing, but clearly the growth curves are coming down to earth. Zhou Xiaochuan, the governor of the People's Bank of China, had to promise the G20 Summit that "volatility is nearing its end." That might or might not be true, but publicly acknowledging volatility would have been almost unthinkable for China even a few years ago. At the same time, Japan, with its iron-fisted central banking system, is looking less like Germany and more like China—pouring heavy stimulus, devaluing the yen, still failing to create more jobs or consumer spending. Corruption and funny-money pranks aren't anomalies in Japan anymore. They are routine. Even in South Korea, where exports have been skyrocketing, life is not as good as was anticipated. Year-on-year exports—memory modules, TVs, computer monitors, Android handsets, the many products of Samsung and LG—are down 14.7 percent, the deepest slump since 2009.

- **American companies and their employees keep getting more productive.** This is the most important one. The manufacturers that have survived are a highly impressive group. Scrappy. Smart. Brave. Not easily spooked or discouraged. Along with some brand-new companies that have joined our early renaissance, we really are "making it in America" these days. We've learned from all the turmoil. Most of us have our acts together now. The numbers bear this out. According to the Economic Policy Institute, worker productivity, defined as the output of goods and services per hours worked, grew by 74 percent between 1973 and 2013. And it's still growing. At the same time, American factories have grown far more efficient, more than offsetting the substantial wage increases we have seen. There are always methods we can incorporate to be even more efficient. Clearly, fresh investment is needed and some work rules could be improved. But I'm convinced: The future of American manufacturing lies in our people working smarter and more effectively than workers anywhere else and being paid for it—not racing to the bottom in wages and other costs. We may never be the cheapest, but we really are the best.

Competitively speaking, we are in a much better place today than we have been in the past few years. There are even some early signs that some jobs may be coming back from overseas, while new ones are being created on American soil. In the scheme of things, the numbers are still small. Sixty thousand manufacturing jobs were added to the U.S. economy in 2014, a fivefold increase of the 12,000 in 2003. In some cases, American companies brought jobs back. In other cases, it's foreign companies (automakers, textile companies, and others) who opened plants here. At the same time, the rate at which jobs are leaving has slowed a bit. One hundred thousand jobs left in 2003. That number was cut to 50,000 in 2014—still 50,000 too many but at least trending in the right direction. And that trend produced the first net increase in twenty years—10,000 additional jobs. No bonanza, but a whole lot better than losing tens or hundreds of thousands of jobs a year. There are some early signs that the tide may actually be turning our way.

A lot of people in our industry used to call me Don Quixote. "There's Bassett," they'd say, "the Man from La Mancha, fighting windmills again." In the past few years, I've had a few of them pull me aside and say, "You are right. We should have done something. We shouldn't have just shut down everything."

When people say, "We can't," I instinctively think, *Oh, yes we can. Just watch*. Not in every instance. Not in the face of irrefutable evidence. Not always. But I've never been one for premature surrender. There's always time for that later on. But guys, let's not turn our backs on this country. Let's keep fighting now. The best really could be yet to come.

YES, IT CAN

Don't ever say America can't achieve impossible goals. And don't underestimate the immense contributions American industry can make. I grew up with all those stories from World War II.

As the Nazi threat was rising in Europe, President Roosevelt went on the radio and, for the first time ever, used the phrase "arsenal of democracy." That's what America had to be, he told the nation that day, December 29, 1940, an arsenal of democracy.

Our troops weren't yet heading off to war. That would come a little more than eleven months later when Pearl Harbor was bombed.

But Roosevelt already realized that America's great industrial capacity would have to be brought into the war effort, the United Kingdom's and inevitably our own.

"The experience of the past two years has proven beyond doubt that no nation can appease the Nazis," he said. "No man can tame a tiger into a kitten by stroking it. There can be no appeasement with ruthlessness. There can be no reasoning with an incendiary bomb."

Our freedom depended on it, he knew. So did the future of future generations. All Americans had to produce, especially those with the means of production in their hands.

It was essential, he said, for American industry to turn all its focus—all of it—away from the luxuries and convenience of civilian life and instead become committed to building the tools of war. I don't believe I've ever heard a politician speak so passionately about industrial output.

"I want to make it clear that it is the purpose of the nation to build now with all possible speed every machine, every arsenal, every factory that we need to manufacture our defense material," he said. "We have the men, the skill, the wealth, and above all, the will. I am confident that if and when production of consumer or luxury goods in certain industries requires the use of machines and raw materials that are essential for defense purposes, then such production must yield, and will gladly yield, to our primary and compelling purpose.

"So I appeal to the owners of plants, to the managers, to the workers, to our own government employees to put every ounce of effort into producing these munitions swiftly and without stint. With this appeal I give you the pledge that all of us who are officers of your government will devote ourselves to the same wholehearted extent to the great task that lies ahead.

"We must be the great arsenal of democracy."

People thought Roosevelt was crazy talking like that. They said Americans would never give up consumer goods for the sake of building more tanks, field tents, and camouflage gear. They said it was impossible to take a roaring civilian economy and, overnight, flip it into a war machine. There was huge skepticism about the nation's ability to meet Roosevelt's goals. Well, guess what? We exceeded virtually every one of them. Americans can achieve miracles when we are inspired to act and the need is great enough.

Will twenty-first-century American manufacturing ever equal that of the mid and late twentieth century, when Roosevelt called the nation together and it really was possible to say, "America makes, the world takes"? Probably not. Today's threats are not the equal of advancing Nazis. We have no Roosevelt, and the world is different today. No one country can possibly dominate the world economy anymore. Technology has made the planet smaller. Globalization is real. Communication is instantaneous. Education is increasingly universal. So is the thirst for freedom. Not one of those genies is going back in the bottle. Other countries have learned to compete with the once-unbeatable United States, and some of them have competitive advantages we are unlikely to reverse.

But still.

I refuse to believe that we don't still have some fight left in us. I refuse to believe that Americans want to shrug and surrender, while these powerful economic engines remain forever in foreign hands. Americans aren't quitters. We weren't quitters in World War II, and we don't have to be today. We really can do this. Vaughan-Bassett has proven that Americans can compete with anyone. The simple answer to the can-it-come-back question is "yes, if . . ."

- Yes, if we make the commitment.
- Yes, if we do the right things.
- Yes, if we change some policies that are holding us back as global competitors.
- And yes, if we take some practical steps to get business and government working together productively again.

There are things we must do and do now. If we take these practical steps, we will compete far more effectively with the nations that have been picking our pockets and eating our lunch. We will promote a renaissance in American manufacturing that can produce millions of new jobs and bring back some of the glory that is truly ours. Here are ten things we need to get started on right now. Some of them are basic. Some are technical. But it's time to get busy on all of them.

- **Keep improving our manufacturing techniques.** America's factories have improved dramatically. We have a right to take pride in that. Our workmanship is superior. Our pace has sped up. Our efficiency is undeniably greater. Our credit and delivery practices have never been better *targeted*. We have created an unprecedented level of teamwork between labor and management. And our reputation, which flows from all the rest of it, is certainly on the rise. "Made in America" is a compliment again, not something anyone needs to be ashamed of. But when it comes to improving the way we do business, these improvements can never stop. We have to keep getting better, week after week, and year after year. Our customers demand it. If we rest on our laurels, our competitors, domestic and foreign, will certainly gain on us. It'll only be a matter of time before we are playing catch-up again. Improve. Improve some more. Keep improving. It's a journey that never ends.

- **Lower the corporate tax rate.** Corporations should pay taxes. I have no problem with that. They benefit from the fruits of America. They should pay their fair share. But what's fair? Do we really need the highest corporate taxes of all the major countries in the world? The current top federal rate, 35 percent, pushes business away. When executives are deciding where to open a new facility, where to expand or where to try something new, that tax rate looms over the decision like a dark shadow, not always determinative but never a help. And don't forget. Many of the states also impose corporate taxes. So the final rate is often higher than whatever the IRS form says. These overly high corporate taxes make us less competitive. It encourages companies to cheat—or at least to use the most aggressive tax-avoidance strategies. It encourages some companies to park their lucrative businesses overseas.

- **Promote repatriation.** That's the word economists use for money that U.S. corporations have parked overseas. There's a huge pile of it right now. Currently, the five hundred largest U.S. companies are hoarding more than $2.1 trillion in foreign banks and investment houses in Bermuda, Ireland, Luxembourg, the Netherlands, the Cayman Islands, and other low-tax countries, avoiding paying the higher U.S. taxes they would owe if they brought the money home. We need to find ways to convince them to repatriate these funds. Offshore American companies should not be given amnesty. There should be incentives to do business in this country instead of other countries. Americans should invest in America. We must have faith in America to be competitive with the rest of the world. That money is doing America no good sitting indefinitely overseas. Apple has the largest offshore pile, $181 billion, according to U.S. Public Interest Research Group. Other big ones include General Electric ($119 billion), Microsoft ($108 billion), and Pfizer ($74 billion). According to filings with the Securities and Exchange Commission, these companies are paying an average of 6 percent in taxes for this money held overseas, compared to the top U.S. rate of 35 percent. The United States should give them a reason to bring this money back now and in the future by lowering our federal corporate tax rate for all U.S. companies operating here and abroad, thus providing an incentive to return the money. Such a policy would help create extra incentives to open future plants in *this* country.

- **Quit signing lopsided trade deals.** Our company supported NAFTA. We supported GATT, which later became the World Trade Organization. My whole life, I have backed the idea of free trade. I don't believe in protectionism. I'm for the freest possible flow of goods around the world. Free trade promotes efficiency and opportunity and lifts the standard of living for people everywhere. That's the theory, anyway. When these massive trade deals came around, our leaders in Washington told us the agreements would open new export markets for American companies. We'd all benefit from an expanding international middle class. Unfortunately, none of that ever came true for us. We were like a lot of American companies.

What we face instead was a flood of new foreign products in the U.S. market, many produced under highly questionable circumstances. Well, free trade has to be fair trade. We can't get fooled again. As Americans assess the Trans-Pacific Partnership and the next generation of international trade deals, we need to be far more skeptical. At a bare minimum, we need tougher enforcement mechanisms and a much more level playing field. Otherwise, no deal.

- **Insist that other countries follow the law.** One of the smartest things our company ever did was also one of the most controversial: bringing the illegal-dumping petition against the Chinese. It taught us free trade will never be fair trade if the other side cheats. In the largest anti-dumping case ever brought against China up to that time, the International Trade Commission confirmed that the Chinese were illegally subsidizing bedroom furniture imports, made them stop, and socked them with millions of dollars in penalties over at least ten years. We proved once and for all that these foreign competitors were not better than we were. Now we have to keep the pressure on. We have to stay vigilant against other nations engaged in similar behavior. In a global economy, there must be rules, and those rules must be followed—by everyone.

- **Remember our competitors aren't all Supermen.** Often, they aren't even Clark Kent. They are other companies, run and staffed by human beings, that have a combination of pluses and minuses that all human enterprises do. That's one of the great advantages of traveling the world and actually visiting other companies. It reminds us: If they can do it, we can probably do it better. We can work harder. We can plan better. We can think deeper. We can care more. Depending on where they are based and who works there, they have certain advantages in the marketplace. Lower wages. Lax regulations. Government subsidies. But in America, we too have advantages. It is our job to discover and exploit them. At Vaughan-Bassett, we have some advantages that give us a real leg up on our competitors who depend on foreign manufacturers. A dedicated, experienced workforce. Physical proximity to our customers. A management team willing to take a risk for something we believe in. Once we figured out how to turn those facts to our advantage, we were off and running and not looking back.

- **Encourage American companies to invest more at home.** It isn't only low wages and tax havens that pull investment away. Many of our laws today actually encourage American companies to take their businesses overseas. We should reverse that pressure with a concerted campaign that rewards domestic investment. One small change that would make a huge difference: speed up the depreciation schedule for new equipment and capital investment. Years ago, when you bought a piece of machinery and it lasted for decades, there was no rush to depreciate its value. Now the rush of technology makes equipment obsolete far more quickly. The IRS's depreciation rules need to catch up to the reality of today. This single change would help to keep American factories up-to-date and encourage our companies to invest more heavily for the long term. If we are going to compete globally today, we have to stay on the technological cutting edge.

- **Turn "Buy American" into more than a slogan.** This starts by reminding Americans how powerful their buying decisions are. Poll after poll shows that most American consumers like products made in America. A walk through the aisles of any big-box store shows that American consumers like a bargain, too, wherever it's made. The question always lingers: Will people pay more for made-in-America? If so, how much more? Or will they just tell pollsters they believe in the principle—then grab whatever is cheapest, without even checking the made-in tag? We need to drag this conversation to the top of the public dialogue. Those of us making-it-in-America need to make sure that everyone knows what we are doing. Government and industry should join together, extolling the virtues of buying high-quality American goods. People need to be constantly reminded of the many benefits our nation receives when we purchase products manufactured here: Fresh dollars bouncing through the economy. Employment for our relatives, neighbors, and friends. A future for our industrial infrastructure. Another small chip in the trade deficit. For those reasons and others, buying American is an act of patriotism today. Americans are a deeply patriotic people. We just have to remind them to be.

- **End the negativity.** It wasn't always the Chinese or the Vietnamese or the Mexicans or the Koreans who hurt American manufacturing. We did a lot of damage to ourselves. We did it by panicking. We did it by lacking faith in ourselves. We did it by thinking we were doomed, often when we weren't doomed at all. We acted like MBAs, not football coaches. We had a losing attitude, so we lost. Going forward, we must do the exact opposite. We have to believe in ourselves and in our people. We have to end the negativity. We have to think and feel and believe like winners. Do that—you'll be surprised just how often you will win.

IT'LL COME BACK IF . . .

- American business leaders and American employees remember we really are in this together. We share far more in common than we have to fight about. We want strong companies with growing business and generous wages and solid security. That will only happen if we build the greatest workplace teams ever—and we can.

- We produce goods and services worthy of the boast "Made in America." We have a great manufacturing tradition in this country. Many of the greatest advances on the assembly line came from American manufacturers. We've built products the whole world is crazy for. We just have to keep doing that—and keep doing it better. If people like what we produce, they will buy it. Truly, that's how business works.

- American consumers join the effort, realizing how very much is at stake. It isn't hard to make a difference. Even a passing thought or an occasional comment would be great. What'll kill us is premature surrender, feeling like America is hopeless, that we're doomed, that our best days are behind, that we can't possibly compete anymore. When Americans join together, we win.

- We reflect for a moment on what made America great. Our strength. Our sense of community. Our refusal to quit. Our support of each other. Our God-given talent. Our hard work. We have it in us. We can do it. We can make it come back.

Conclusion

Future Vision

Business has to be about something more than cutting expenses, raising margins, and avoiding taxes. No matter how you slice it, business is still about people in the end.

America, I believe, is something special, and it's worth passing on.

For some time, I had been trying to think of the right way to share that passion with the next generations in my family. I knew it would take more than my telling another long-winded story after Sunday dinner or suggesting an inspiring book to read or dragging the grandkids to hear me give a speech. I would have to come up with something they could all relate to.

Then, I got an idea. Last year, I decided to take all seventeen members of my immediate family—my wife and I, our three children and their spouses, and all nine grandchildren—on a trip to Normandy, France.

I'd been to Normandy before. It would be wonderful if all Americans got that chance. I am not aware of a place, here or abroad, that better exemplifies the extraordinary bravery, sacrifice, and commitment that Americans are capable of.

I told my family: "I'm not sure all of you know what your country has done for you. I don't want to die before you all get to see Normandy."

Normandy isn't just an idea or piece of history or abstract symbol of some sort. It's a real place. You can go there. You can see it. You can walk around. You can learn about what happened in June 1944 and how it changed the future of the world. You can react. You can let it change you.

And so we made the trip. We flew to Paris and drove about three hours to the northern coast of France, where rocky beaches and cliffs of granite and limestone tumble into the choppy English Channel. My family heard the unforgettable story of what happened there.

As World War II raged on, German troops occupied a broad swath of France. It was horrible. For four long years, the French people suffered unspeakably at the hands of the Nazis. Tanks in the streets. Firefights and bombardments. Jews and others sent to their deaths in concentration camps. By the spring of 1944, Allied troops—American, British, and Canadian—were amassing for an invasion across the channel. Their target: the five beaches of Normandy, code-named Sword, Juno, Gold, Omaha, and Utah. The first wave of the landing, which came to be called D-Day, was set for June 5, 1944.

The Germans were dug in tight. They had high emplacements along the cliffs and many other advantages: four army divisions, a natural wall fortified with tank-top turrets and extensive barbed wire, a large storehouse of vehicles and arms, the notoriously rotten weather, and a treacherous channel the invaders had to cross.

But cross the Allies did—exactly twenty-four hours later than planned—throwing everything they had at the waiting enemy. It began with moonlight parachute jumps and glider landings, quickly followed by massive naval bombardments and air attacks. As dawn broke, the amphibious landings began. Thousands and thousands of American troops leapt into the water and ran ashore as comrades to the left and right of them were cut down by enemy fire. There were so many bodies floating in the water, the arriving troops literally had to climb over them, as German firepower kept raining down like a deluge. It went on like that for hours and then days. Behind them came land forces deployed from bases along the south coast of England.

It was the largest amphibious invasion in the history of warfare, nearly 150,000 Allied troops on the first day alone, fully half of them Americans. As the Battle of Normandy pressed on, that total would rise past one million supported by 148,000 vehicles, 570,000 tons of supplies, 6,939 vessels: 1,213 warships, 4,126 transport vessels, and 736 ancillary craft and 864 merchant vessels. This was big.

Progress was slow. It wasn't until June 12 that all five beachheads were taken and connected. Omaha Beach was the worst bloodbath. Despite heavy losses, the Allied forces just kept coming, refusing to back down, gradually expanding their territory over the months to come.

Historians call it the first successful opposed landings across the English Channel in eight centuries. It led to the ending of most of Germany's occupation of France and the establishment of a crucial new front for the Allies. What started on D-Day ended with the liberation of Paris and the restoration of the French Republic. It was an undeniable turning point in the war. If the Battle of Normandy had been a failure instead of a bloody, glorious success— who knows? The French today might well be *spreken ze deutsch* along the banks of the Seine.

But there was no misunderstanding the terrible price. Allied casualties topped 10,000, more than 6,600 of them Americans. In all, 4,414 were confirmed dead.

THE ULTIMATE SACRIFICE, THE GREATEST LESSON

On our family visit, we walked together through the Normandy American Cemetery in Colleville-sur-Mer. Situated on a bluff overlooking Omaha Beach, it's a vast and somber place, 172 acres in all, rows and rows of identical whitewashed crosses and a few Stars of David. Each grave is marked simply with the name, unit, date of birth, and date of death of the service member buried there.

With my wife, children, and grandchildren, I took all this in. Even though I'd been there before, I still found that cemetery incredibly moving. The scale of it. The mission the fallen were pursuing. Their willingness to give everything for their nation and all it stood for.

Then we went to one of the British cemeteries.

The British don't have one big cemetery like the Americans do. They have several smaller cemeteries. With Britain right across the channel from Normandy, the Brits could more easily take their dead back home. Not as many are buried in Normandy, though some of them are. The British cemetery we visited, the Bayeux War Cemetery, I believe is the largest one. In many ways, it is similar to the American cemetery. Same somber feeling. Same dignified simplicity. But the British do one thing differently. Each British cross is engraved not just with the person's name, unit insignia, and dates of birth and death. It also included the fallen service member's age.

Eighteen. Nineteen. Twenty. Twenty-one. Hardly any had even seen thirty when they were cut down in battle.

God, they were all so young!

Wyatt's three sons—Elliott, Spencer, and Huntley—and Fran's son, Ashton, were all in their late teens or early twenties. They were standing quietly off to the side when suddenly it dawned on them. The young men in these graves were hardly any older than they were. It stunned them. It positively stunned them. The American soldiers were just as young. But their ages were not inscribed on the crosses, and nobody took time to do the math. Seeing the ages of the British soldiers finally made everything seem real to those boys. They couldn't help but filter it through their own young minds.

I was standing behind them. I walked up slowly and put my hands on their shoulders.

"Gentlemen," I said, "would you be willing to do this for your country?"

They just stared into the distance as I walked away.

When they finally turned away, all of them had looks of shock on their faces. It had never occurred to them that young men their ages had given their lives for our freedom.

It was worth the whole trip right there.

EVER ONWARD

As this long journey of mine has unfolded, I am more convinced than I have ever been: It's time we all fall in love with our country again.

America deserves it. So do we. Honestly, where else would *you* rather live?

Normandy was a powerful reminder of that, just as John Kennedy's admonition and George Patton's drive and Winston Churchill's strategic brilliance and my grandfather's business acumen were. Some values are worth fighting for, and we Americans are blessed with many of them.

This effort to save our company, this desire to support our communities, this commitment to keep American men and women employed—it all flows from my abiding belief that America stands for something worth saving and worth passing along.

- The importance of high-quality craftsmanship.
- The exchange of value for a dollar.
- The knowledge that our team members have our backs and we always have theirs.
- The responsibility to support our own economy and demand a level international playing field.
- The need to invest in our future and maintain the infrastructure that our ancestors have passed along.
- The duty to leave this earth better off than we found it.
- The understanding that sometimes we have to *be* the change, not just respond to it.
- The eternal openness to outside people and goods, balanced by an equally strong support for our own.
- The recognition that numbers matter, but people matter even more.
- The belief in lifelong service, not entitlement.
- The extraordinary power of one.

That's the America I love and feel deeply indebted to. Isn't that a place worth loving and fighting for? I hate to see her greatness degraded.

I get exasperated when I see people thinking only of themselves. I don't understand the coarseness and the lack of respect some people have for their own fellow workers. Business has to be about something more than cutting expenses, raising margins, and avoiding taxes. No matter how you slice it, business is still about people in the end. Treat them decently, and you'll get the best out of them. How can you look people in the eye and send their jobs overseas without giving them a chance to prove themselves? Do you really think Americans are incapable of competing with anyone in the world? Shouldn't American workers get the opportunity to try? Too many companies hardly talk to their people, never saying, "This is what we have to do." It's time for us to put people back in the formula. This is a joint venture, America is. We're in it together. All of us.

Decades later, I still haven't shaken that Hong Kong factory owner out of my head. "The greediest people we ever met," he said of Americans. He might have been right about some of them, but I refuse to believe those are the ones who truly represent us. I refuse to believe we can't do better than that.

I know Helen and Linda. I know the people in the Vaughan-Bassett finishing room and on the conveyor belt. There are people just like them all across the United States. I know the retailers who stock our furniture and the people who take it home and make it part of their lives. I know my family, and I know families across America.

We aren't quitters. We work hard and refuse to give up. Wherever we come from, wherever we're going, we don't crawl over each other to get there.

America, who are we today? That's the final question.

We are Americans, the children of a country we can't help loving, the carriers of a vision that can never be allowed to die.

Acknowledgments

This book would not have been written without the insistence and encouragement of my agent, Peter McGuigan, at Foundry Literary + Media, and his colleague, Kirsten Neuhaus, who led me through the intricacies of finding a publisher, signing contracts, and hiring a ghostwriter, and who freely offered additional advice and patience to someone who had no idea what it took to write a book.

I will always be appreciative of the training I've received from my lifelong employers, Vaughan-Bassett Furniture Company and The Bassett Furniture Industries, who not only taught me the tools of the trade but also paid for many of my earlier mistakes.

I've had the limitless support of my entire family—my bride, Pat, who tolerated long absences while I was at my desks in Roaring Gap and Hobe Sound; my daughter, Fran, who enhanced this project with her many suggestions; and of course my sons, Doug and Wyatt. Wyatt again led me through the legal minutiae of tippability and Doug, an English major at the University of Virginia, taught me to organize my thoughts and tell this story.

My deepest appreciation goes to Kate Hartson, executive editor for my publisher, who supervised and suggested many revisions and additions to this project. Patsy Jones, marketing and publicity director for the Hachette Book Group, literally taught me how to sell books. Thanks as well to James Gregorio, Janis Spidel, and Roberta Teer for their excellent contributions.

My staff at Vaughan-Bassett Furniture Company was always there for any information I needed—Andy Williamson, Curtis Carrico, Rick Harrison, Joyce Phillips, Doug Brannock, and Jim Stout, supported by Jim Underwood, John Crookshanks, Roxanna Funk, Marsha Lawson, Missy Carico, and Kathy Alderman.

Our group of lawyers at King & Spalding—Joe Dorn, Michael Taylor, and Bonnie Byers—was always on hand to provide important international trade figures.

To all the many factory workers who taught me this business over the past fifty years, thank you and Godspeed.

Frankly, there would be no book without my assistant, Sheila Key. Sheila typed, suggested, and corrected, and kept me organized and on schedule. I can't thank her enough.

Ellis Henican was introduced to me by Peter McGuigan to be my ghostwriter. He became much more, prying out of me creativity I didn't know I had. What I expected to be a long slog turned into a labor of love. Thank you, Ellis!